MOVING FORWARD

The Power of Consistent Choices in Everyday Life

PETER NIEMAN

BALBOA.
PRESS
A DIVISION OF HAY HOUSE

Balboa Press books may be ordered through booksellers or by contacting:

Balboa Press
A Division of Hay House
1663 Liberty Drive
Bloomington, IN 47403
www.balboapress.com
1 (877) 407-4847

Because of the dynamic nature of the Internet, any web addresses or links contained in this book may have changed since publication and may no longer be valid. The views expressed in this work are solely those of the author and do not necessarily reflect the views of the publisher, and the publisher hereby disclaims any responsibility for them.

The author of this book does not dispense medical advice or prescribe the use of any technique as a form of treatment for physical, emotional, or medical problems without the advice of a physician, either directly or indirectly. The intent of the author is only to offer information of a general nature to help you in your quest for emotional and spiritual well-being. In the event you use any of the information in this book for yourself, which is your constitutional right, the author and the publisher assume no responsibility for your actions.

Any people depicted in stock imagery provided by Thinkstock are models, and such images are being used for illustrative purposes only.
Certain stock imagery © Thinkstock.

Print information available on the last page.

ISBN: 978-1-5043-3248-4 (sc)
ISBN: 978-1-5043-3250-7 (hc)
ISBN: 978-1-5043-3249-1 (e)

Library of Congress Control Number: 2015907404

Balboa Press rev. date: 05/07/2015

CONTENTS

ACKNOWLEDGMENTS

Lao Tzu wrote in the *Tao Te Ching* that a journey of a thousand miles begins with a single step. In writing this book, I owe much to my teachers and those who supported me in this joyous journey of moving forward. Since starting with that single first step, I can clearly see that moving forward requires a community, each of us supporting one another.

Editing an avalanche of ideas took patience, dedication, and discipline. My deepest and sincerest gratitude goes out to my excellent editors. I honor the divine in you.

What was supposed to be a *lunch* to simply catch up became a *launch* of the final drafts of *Moving Forward*. Dave Irvine inserted an *a* in the word *lunch* by offering to keep me *a*ccountable. Dave, I respect you and look forward to your many books yet to come. You are a blessing to your fellow travelers as you continue to remind us that love never fails. You taught me much about simple living in a complex world.

Lao Tzu also taught me the value of balanced living and inspired me to equally honor all three areas that matter so much to me—mind, body, and spirit.

My spiritual mentors continue to inspire me every moment as I move forward. I am grateful to Dr. Len Zoeteman, Ray Matheson, Randy Carter, Dr. Norman Vincent Peale, Rick Warren, Alan Cohen, Davidji, Robert Holden, and Dr. Wayne Dyer.

My soul continues to be stirred daily by the timeless truths taught by Dale Carnegie. I owe a deep gratitude to John and Faye Fisher. And to Paul Gaudet, my instructor, thanks for believing in me.

My mind has been kept curious as a result of associating with Jim Rohn and Zig Ziglar. Long after they have departed, they continue to help millions of others move forward.

Recording ideas for this book was a joy, using all the fine writing instruments I purchased from Moses Valdez at O'Hare Airport's Montblanc store. Thank you, my friend, for your excellent salesmanship.

Thanks to the bellman at the Montelucia Resort who offered me a bottle of cool water after a long run in the Arizona heat. You taught me to keep kindness simple by striving to honor the needs of others.

Running every day of my life allows me to generate ideas for future books. To Grant Molyneaux, my coach and Boston Marathon motivator, my sincere thanks. Supporting my feet for decades has been a shoe company with a slogan that says it all—Just Do It. Thanks to Nike Canada who sent me a free pair of running shoes when I shared my intent to run one hundred marathons by age sixty. Like Dallas-based Dr. Ken Cooper, another mentor, I too shall keep at least one pair of shoes as a reminder that marathon running is more than running—it's a lifestyle we *intentionally* choose.

Music by the Eagles, during many hours of running, inspired many ideas in this book. On more than one occasion I learned that we can still be in chains even if we have the keys to unlock those chains. I was often reminded to "Take It Easy."

Staying nutritionally fit was never easy for the first forty marathons, and then I met the Juice Plus Company. Thanks for keeping my free radicals well below the danger zone! Thanks also to Dr. Bill Sears, who always will remain a role model when it comes to creative writing.

By divine design I am able to regularly do what I enjoy so much—part-time journalism. Thanks to the *Globe and Mail*, which allowed me to share my ideas nationally. To my editor at the *Calgary Herald*, Tom Babin, thanks for putting so much of your trust in me. You continue to encourage me. The frequent e-mails praising my balanced contributions mean a lot. Thanks also to CTV for allowing me to play with you in a sandbox I can never get tired of. To QR77 radio, the number seven was almost perfect—I learned much.

My deep gratitude goes out to World Vision, an organization that allowed me to join Team World Vision. By doing so, I am allowed to serve others by running marathons. All my future marathons will raise money to help children in the poorest parts of this planet avoid death from starvation.

And then there were some who did their best to derail my destiny. Later I found out they were my toughest teachers on purpose, angels sent into my life to teach me what I needed to learn. I send you love.

To my wife and best friend, I can only say that you are a gift from above, and moving forward together with you has allowed me to see the eyes of God. To our four kids, thank you for being so different in the various ways you decided to move on. You have reminded me why patience is mentioned first when the Bible describes love. My parents supported me in so many ways. When I look back, I realize daily as a pediatrician that my happy childhood was a unique privilege.

And finally I honor my creator, the spirit of truth. Without God, my senior partner, this book would never have been born. The rainbow on the front page is there for a reason. It is summarized by two life-changing words: unfailing love.

If what I've written in the pages to follow resonates with you, the reader, do not thank me, but thank the great teacher who arrived when the student was ready.

INTRODUCTION

Perhaps you feel stuck in a rut. You may be lacking inner peace. Or maybe you cannot let go of a painful past that imprisons you daily. You may be completely unsure of your purpose. You may feel unloved. You may feel as if disappointments will never stop devouring you. Perhaps your mind used to be filled with curiosity, but now it lacks vigor. Others may honor you, but you do not honor yourself. You are stuck. Moving forward seems so unlikely. Or … maybe you have moved forward but feel there is more to life.

What I am about to share comes from a place of humility. I did not decide to write this book to impress anyone with how much I know as a doctor, a part-time medical journalist, or an endurance athlete.

My motive is to help you and inspire you to live your life in such a way that when you cross the finish line one day, you can look back and say, "I served well and reached my purpose." It has been said that there are two important days in anyone's life: the day you were born and the day you figure out why.

> It has been said that there are two important days in anyone's life: the day you were born and the day you figure out why.

I wrote this book to encourage you on the journey we all share—the path forward. We all get to choose how we want to move forward. Moving forward one step at a time is indeed a process, a journey, and it takes a lifetime. Sometimes this journey will be marked by detours. Be patient and trust that, as the poem "Desiderata" reminds us, the universe will unfold as it should.

Many of the ideas in this book will resonate almost immediately; other will make perfect sense only later—perhaps after a sudden setback or a deep disappointment. As the Zen saying goes, when the student is ready, the teacher arrives. That has been very true in my own life and in the lives of many others who have experienced enlightenment episodes, one after another. This shedding of new light can also be described as an inner knowing, a quantum moment, a major, unexpected shift.

I have intentionally kept my writing simple; I've filled these words with a deep sense of humility, and I deliver these thoughts with compassion. I can share only what I have learned over the years through adversity. Most of these afflictions were overcome because I learned what it means to move forward. Looking back, I can confidently say that those lessons—the roses and the thorns—all arrived at the perfect time and that there are no accidents. During the darkest adversities this was hard to see. But every person I met and every situation I experienced taught me something. I had the choice to learn and get better or to ignore events as random coincidences. I chose to grow from adversity.

The theme of this book is that we all get to choose how we want to move forward. Moving forward requires an alive and open heart.

People who have decided to move forward may look like this:

- They radiate inner peace, contentment, serenity, and tranquility in the midst of life's many adversities.
- They are aware that a highly energized life leads to being more productive. This productivity is not just for selfish reasons but for sharing with those in need. The ripple of moving forward touches others. When we give ourselves to other, we experience healing.
- They see daily discipline not as a form of self-inflicted masochistic suffering but as a pathway to a place of purpose and service. It's a commitment to living one's destiny in abundance—not in lack.
- They have discovered that consistency in moving forward creates a higher level of vitality and inner harmony. A commitment to daily actions over decades not only teaches us about a compound

effect but also helps us to stay content, because we know our purpose.

- They understand that it is possible to move forward alone but that in the end it is our associations that change everything. The company we keep determines who we become. Associations are roots that influence the fruits.
- They enjoy the bliss of an inner, serene knowing that faith is simply a form of trusting in the wisdom of a divine intelligence. This higher power cannot be touched and can only be known fully when we love others *as* we love ourselves.
- They are motivated by love, kindness, and compassion.
- They understand there is a simple eternal truth that has been taught for centuries. It is all about how to live life purposefully: don't do bad things; always do good things.

You may notice I listed eight qualities of people who choose to move forward. Why eight? The number symbolizes infinity. There is an infinite number of ways to move forward, but in the end we get to choose the way that resonates best with who we are. We were made by our source for a purpose, and to find that place of calling is pure joy and peace.

It is with a deep sense of gratitude that I get to honor you by sharing these suggestions. May you receive some benefits from these words, may a new mind transform you, and may these pages inspire you to move forward all the days of your life. We are about to embark together on a journey I have called *Moving Forward.*

CHAPTER 1

ADVERSITY

I have always faced adversity, but it has brought
something out of me, and made me a success.
—J. C. Penney

I honor adversity as a gift to help me grow.
—Alan Cohen

It was two days before the Houston Marathon. I came home one evening from the TV studio where I am a regular panelist on health matters. I was in a great mood. The show had gone well; my answers had been brief, informative, and entertaining. Once we had gone off the air, I'd felt a higher energy in the studio. This energy had lingered long after the bright lights had been dimmed. During the segment I had tried hard to do what Franklin D. Roosevelt said: "Be sincere; be brief; be seated." That advice had worked well.

As soon as I returned home, I spotted my dog, Sage, a huge, gentle, and energetic black Labrador. Sage has been blessed with an amazing attitude. This enables her to live a zestful life. In many ways she is one of my best teachers. From her body language I could tell she was ready for a walk.

Soon after we headed outdoors into the cool, dark night, Sage spotted a rabbit. Fortunately for the rabbit, Sage was on a leash. I had no choice but to pick up the pace a bit as she forcefully strained in the direction of the rabbit. Unfortunately, she gained momentum, and soon I was pulled over, losing my grip on the uneven, slippery snow beneath my running shoes.

In the slowest of slow motions, I saw myself fly through the air and land hard on my left hip and shoulder. It was a nightmare. I could hardly stand on my left leg—and a marathon was forty-eight hours away! I limped home with Sage walking next to me, woefully looking into my eyes as if to say, "Sorry about that, but I could not help it, because that is what dogs do."

Fast-forward to Houston a few days later, and I held the finisher's medal in my hand. I was still limping but had covered the 26.2 miles anyhow, guided by a heart-rate monitor and enduring excruciating pain and discomfort for close to four hours.

When I flew back to Canada, I reflected on what had happened. Adversity has the potential to teach us lessons when we remain open to learn them. In this case, I was reminded that when we set goals in life and prepare for the right moment, we may face sudden setbacks. We then get to decide whether we go ahead, push hard, and give it our best shot or drop out, even before the race has started.

Inspired by the J. C. Penney quote at the start of the chapter, I chose to do my best, even though I knew it wouldn't be my best result. I have learned that too many people will not start something unless it is perfect. By living their lives this way, they miss out on some great adventures, challenges, and opportunities.

Those who wait for life to be perfect before they move forward remind me of a great poem by Leonard Cohen:

> Ring the bells that still can ring
> Forget your perfect offering.
> There is a crack in everything.
> That is how the light gets in.

The story of my injured days before an important marathon is rather simple, but it makes the point of how life can be perfect one moment, like a plane flying smoothly, and then suddenly, we encounter unexpected turbulence. We are suddenly shaken in all directions, wondering if our bumpy ride will somehow become smooth again—or maybe not. All of us, sooner or later, will face the shock of sudden change. Fear knocks at our door. I am reminded of the quote "Fear knocked at the door. Faith answered and no one was there." The problem, though, is that far too often fear comes back and knocks again.

Things went from bad to worse after the marathon: the electronic health records in my medical clinic caused major troubles; my favorite fountain pen's nib got damaged; my four kids, one after the other, caught viral infections; my wife was in a bad mood, fighting her own obstacles; and bills were ballooning all at once. I felt I was under an attack with all these events adding up together and causing unpleasant, unexpected obstacles in my life. These were not just a bend in my road; they were bumps, bouncing me all over the place, one after another.

While facing these challenges, I was reminded of these words, which synchronistically showed up at *just* the right moment: "When life presents challenges and we are able to utilize them, we are wise." It has been stated that we profit from our pain when we advance from our adversity. I could truly understand what these words meant because of my personal experiences.

To utilize adversity is not easy. It requires a patient persistence. President Calvin Coolidge said, "Nothing in the world can take the place of persistence. Talent will not; nothing is more common than unsuccessful men with talent. Genius will not; the world is full of educated derelicts. Persistence and determination alone are omnipotent."

Various kinds of relentless adversities seem to strike us all at once, one problem after another. It seems like waves crashing repeatedly against rocks by the edge of the ocean. The writer C. S. Lewis said that "hardships often prepare ordinary people for an extraordinary destiny." I am convinced from my experiences as a physician that hardships indeed prepare many of us for a destiny far bigger than we can imagine at our time of pain.

Scripture calls these hardships *trials*. The Bible goes on to even say, "Consider it all *joy*, knowing that the testing of one's faith delivers patience." (James 1:2 NKJV, emphasis mine) Most of us do not choose adversity as the avenue to joy! Instead, we tend to fear hardships and avoid them at all costs. We may even question the reasons for our hardships by asking, "Why me?" In a fit of anger we may even shout, "Life is not fair!"

Plenty of people have read Rabbi Harold Kushner's book *When Bad Things Happen to Good People*. I suspect many of those readers felt they had made a deal with God, believing that they would be protected from pressures as long as they obeyed the rules. But this is not how God operates. We all experience cares, difficulties, and troubles—life is impermanent, and it evolves constantly. At some point all of us get an invitation to view adversities as our best teachers. Nobody is immune. Surrendering to the fact that we are not in full control, we grow from adversities and move forward after painful experiences.

When we grow from adversity, we become wise. Pain should never be allowed to go to waste. As someone observed, "Progress without pain is not possible." We move forward when we allow adversity to deliver life's lessons; pain has the potential to make us more resilient; our level of insight, enlightenment, and awareness increase. Like trees buffeted by storms, our root system deepens when we face challenges, but only if we surrender and remain openhearted. It is when trees resist storms that their branches break.

One outstanding advantage of adversity, soaring far above the other benefits, is the lesson that our pain produces compassion. Overcoming adversity by moving forward makes us more compassionate toward others who face similar awful experiences.

We all may have different stories, but basically they are the same: *everyone* encounters problems. Problems often pounce on us when we least expect them. It is as if the stories of our lives read like happy novels, but then a sudden shift in the next chapter turns things upside down. Pema Chodron, a well-respected Buddhist nun, uses the analogy of a bird being thrown from a nest all of a sudden; the comfort of the warm nest is gone *in an instant*.

Sooner or later we discover life's impermanence. The very vicissitudes we read about in the lives of others suddenly strike us, apparently from nowhere, and shake us like a hunting dog violently shakes its prey, freshly trapped between its clenched jaws.

Life Is like a Grindstone

Motivational speaker and best-selling author, Zig Ziglar once observed, "Life is like a grindstone. Whether it wears you down or polishes you up depends on what you are made of."

Will you allow adversity to wear you down or polish you up? This decision becomes the fork in the road where we have to make a choice: it can keep us stuck in dark depression and even cause us to slowly slide backward, or it can propel us forward. Our attitudes toward adversity become our quantum moments (moments we never forget, because they impact the trajectory of our lives *forever*). Our perspective determines whether we grow bitter or better. That is what this chapter is all about.

> **Will you allow adversity to wear you down or polish you up?**

Adversity reveals what we are made of in terms of our endurance and patience. We discover *where* and *when* our endurance has its limits. It is often during adversity that we discover what our assets are and also what our weaknesses and limitations are. A painful crisis can teach us that we do not have as much control as our "sophisticated" egos would have us believe. (In this book when I use the word *ego*, I use it in the context being singularly self-centered. Whenever I see the word *ego*, it reminds me of Dr. Wayne Dyer's definition: edging God out.)

Adversity can polish us up by forcing us to ask deep questions about the roots of our suffering. We may wrestle with what I call, "the tough questions triggered by tough times." We may resist dealing with these questions. Or we can learn the lessons delivered to our inbox—lessons customized just for us with our address written in bold letters. When we are on the grindstone, getting polished by life's adversities, various questions swirl through our troubled minds.

Some may start by questioning the role of God. Some spiritual seekers assert that God causes adversity. They blame God for adversity or at least claim that He allows it for a specific purpose. God did it for a reason, and His wisdom never fails. "He is sovereign," they tell people facing pain. "Therefore we must simply trust His decisions for both the good and the bad in our lives." Many of us may make our best efforts to see the hand of God in our suffering. But what does the word *God* mean?

When the word *God* is mentioned in the Alcoholics Anonymous twelve-step program, it is followed by *"as we understand Him."* After many years of studying spirituality, I have concluded that God is too complex to fully understand. It is that simple. No human being shall ever fully understand God. The key word here is *fully*. I suppose some are extremely developed in their faith, but at best they understand only a *part* of God. Nobody understands God fully. Nobody can claim that he or she is God's counselor. We refer to God as a higher power because God's unfathomable ways are far deeper than our limited ways, far higher than our highest IQ, and far wider than our wonderful wisdom.

What about those of us who are deeply offended by the word *God*? For some, God does not exist. Engaging in questions about God is a waste of time. In fact, the idea of God frankly angers many. Instead of trying to figure God out, some say, "It's a waste of time to think too much. Just endure." They claim, "Every negative has a root somewhere. Let's find it and deal with it." They add, "Keep a stiff upper lip; keep calm and move forward." To them life just happens; every event unfolds simply by coincidence after coincidence after coincidence after coincidence; all of these events happen *completely* by chance. "It's all random," they declare with calm conviction in their voices.

I am not sure anyone understands *exactly* what the correct answer may be when we search for the roots of our inevitable suffering. We may never agree on the roots. But for some of us, the reality is that adversities squeezed us like a tightly coiled python until we were brought to a place of surrendering to a higher power. Like an addict, we realize that we are powerless and that it is time to surrender to a force infallible in its intelligence.

> **I am not sure anyone understands exactly what the correct answer may be when we search for the roots of our inevitable suffering.**

People of various philosophies often sense the love and provision of an invisible force at work during their deepest, darkest times. For some of us it takes many storms to learn this single lesson. We may be shocked to the core at first, overflowing with deep sorrow and struggling as we resist the inevitable. The ultimate path to peace is surrender. Some call it the art of allowing. Others may refer to it as being detached from the outcome.

One way to process adversity is to consider that when it happens, we have the *choice* of deciding to grow from it or allow it to ruin our lives. It can polish us up or wear us down. Will we learn the lessons we are destined to learn when we suffer?

How we handle obstacles in life determines who we become. Adversity transforms us, and as a caterpillar is transformed into a butterfly, once we are truly transformed, we can never go back to being a caterpillar. It is not a mere change; it is a profound transformation. Adversity shapes our character *only* if we allow it to prune and polish us.

Booker T. Washington once said, "Success is not to be measured by the position someone has reached in life, but the obstacles he has overcome while trying to succeed." It has also been said that the record books do not keep records of the score at half time. So never base how you will finish on how well you are doing somewhere along your struggles. Stay patient as you are polished and pruned by life's challenges. To be patient is hard; not being patient is harder in the long run.

> **Success is not to be measured by the position someone has reached in life, but the obstacles he has overcome while trying to succeed.**
> **—Booker T. Washington**

An Idea While Running in the Snow

Not so long ago, I went outside early one dark, stormy morning and was surprised by snowflakes, driven at ninety-degree angles into my exposed face. Although an arctic air mass had plunged temperatures far below freezing, I was glad I'd decided to head outside, because within thirty minutes of my run, I heard in my consciousness, *How long will it last?* At that time, a time of facing one of the worst storms in my life, I felt as if the *only* thing that kept me sane while I was going through hell and back was my morning runs.

If we were to look back at some of our disappointments and frustrations, we have to admit that many arrived unexpectedly but that the vast majority had a shelf life. They passed in the end. Problems pass just like the snowstorm from that memorable morning run.

I read somewhere that a man kept a picture of a boat stranded on a beach above his desk in his office. The picture was captioned "The tide always comes back." That image can become a meaningful metaphor for many of our troubles.

> **The tide always comes back. This too shall pass ...**

Many problems are only temporary. You can say, "This too shall pass." I have learned two simple truths when trouble strikes:

- Ask what lesson this experience will teach you.
- Know that all troubles eventually pass when we either die or adjust to what is. Nothing should disturb or dismay us.

Becoming Left-Handed in a Hurry

It is important to remind ourselves that some adversity is self-inflicted.

A few years ago I was forced to become left-handed for a few weeks due to a splinted finger on my right hand. The tendon by the tip of my finger had snapped apart when I had bent the finger the wrong way as a result of getting it caught while hurriedly getting dressed one day. I have observed that numerous "accidents" are a result of being in a hurry or being fatigued and thus losing focus.

My wife saw the commotion and said, "You have a mallet finger." I Googled it, and she was right. I had a mallet finger. It meant a splint for six weeks straight—not even for a second could I take the finger out of the splint. But the tide came back. Eventually this also passed. Today I can look at my finger, and there is not even a sign of that damage. It is 100 percent healed and functions like new.

I experienced another self-inflicted adversity because of my marathon-running habits. Although I have been running approximately 3,500 kilometers each year since 1992, I pushed hard in my training and ignored all my years of experience while I was in training for one of my favorite marathons. Experts say to gradually increase distances after a layoff. My enthusiasm to run a Boston Marathon–qualifying time in Texas led me to run too far too soon during my training, and as a result I got injured. I finished the race in Houston significantly slower than expected. This was a huge setback; I became a patient instead of a Boston Marathon runner at that time.

After two months of therapy and dialing down my running significantly, I recovered 100 percent. The tide came back, and the low tide that had stranded the boat on the beach transformed into the high tide that floated that boat back into the ocean.

Ten Lessons from Marathon Running

What does it take to overcome obstacles? Over the past twenty-two years I have had the honor to run many marathons. At the time of this writing, I am getting closer to my goal of completing my one hundredth marathon. I have run these events all over the world. I ran my only ultramarathon at the tip of Africa as a way to welcome the new millennium. It was a fifty-six-kilometer race over many hills under the blazing African sunshine, but the stunning views of deep, blue, sparkling ocean compensated for the symbolic ups and downs of ultrarunning.

I have also done the famous Boston Marathon a few times and struggled, significantly slower than usual, across the finish line of the New York City Marathon, which ends in Central Park. I love this race so much I told my wife that when the time comes one day to scatter my ashes, she has to do it at the finish line of this iconic race!

I can honestly say that the journey more than the destination has taught me the most. The numerous medals at home remind me that I am a finisher, but what it took to get there matters far more. The longer I run, the more meaningful this reminder by Sara Teasdale has become: "I make the most of all that comes and the least of all that goes."

There are at least ten lessons I learned that have helped me overcome the obstacle of completing 26.2 miles close to a hundred times. It is an obstacle often compounded by heat, wind, rain, snow, sleet, hills, floods, and humidity.

Although running marathons generated these lessons, you need not be an endurance athlete to appreciate them yourself.

1. Always be prepared.
2. Have a positive, realistic reason for doing what you are doing. Pure motives are powerful forces that allow us to overcome adversity and afflictions.
3. Believe that you are able to handle most obstacles. You have what it takes.
4. Take a huge obstacle and break it down into small steps.
5. Every problem has a solution ultimately. Finding it requires patience.
6. Have a written plan of how you will tackle your troubles, and review this plan often, ideally every day.
7. Be consistent.
8. Refuse to lose hope. Endure endlessly.
9. Appreciate the help you get from those who celebrate and align with your intention. Supporters sustain us when we are experiencing the inevitable storms of an impermanent, chaotic life. Sweating becomes sweeter with the enthusiastic support of spectators along the pathways of the tough battles we must endure.
10. Ultimately faith is the confidence that you can fully trust a creator god or higher power who will help you overcome your challenges and turn setbacks into comebacks.

The Olympics as a Teacher

Since adversities so often strike with no warning, preparation is key. This preparation is not about expecting negatives. It is simply a mature knowing that in this life we *will* all face adversity at some point. If we are to move forward, we need one single quality first and foremost: *resilience*. A wise teacher once said that we either are in the middle of a storm, heading into a storm, or just coming out of one. It has also been said that when we are drowning, it is too late to take swimming lessons.

My wife loves watching the Olympic Games every two years. For her it's a good thing that the Winter and Summer Olympics have been spaced in such a manner that every two years there is an Olympic event. Over the years I have been infected by her enthusiasm for following all kinds of athletes compete against all odds against the best of the best on the world stage.

The famous Olympian sprinter Jesse Owens once said, "The battles that count aren't the ones for gold medals. The struggles within yourself—the invisible, inevitable battles inside all of us—that is where it is at."

Every Olympic event seems to include athletes who overcame adversity by preparing for years in advance, not only in a physical realm but also working on a rigorous mental regime. A swimmer takes up swimming as a result of being diagnosed as an asthmatic. A young man loses both legs due to a rare genetic abnormality and competes with the best on prosthetic legs. A loved one dies days before the Olympics, and the athlete wins a gold medal in memory of a departed relative.

How do these amazing athletes do this? They become resilient by relentless preparation, day in and day out. Their fortitude and patience allow them to conquer challenges. They associate with key people, stay focused, never give up, guard their energy, and move forward incrementally to the very top.

We Must Have a Reason

Every year I learn from Jeff Roberti, a former waiter who today is a multimillionaire. He runs his own company that promotes fruit and vegetable consumption via capsules. This product has helped Jeff overcome financial obstacles and turned him into a teacher, motivator, and businessman.

Instead of staying static as a struggling waiter, he has become a passionate person. When Jeff talks about his passions, there is a delightful glow in his eyes. His whole being beams energy, serving and helping others to constantly grow. Wherever his travels take him, and he travels virtually nonstop, he is always fueled by this powerful purpose. His business allows him to feel significant, not because he is so successful but because he instills hope in others that *they too* can move forward from poverty to having a fulfilling purpose. Jeff lives by the motto "Love all; serve all."

I usually am in the audience twice a year at nutrition conferences where Jeff has the crowds in the palm of his hand. It's a real treat to look at the audience and see them warm up to Jeff's inspirational teaching.

I have heard him talk so often that I can predict the climax of each talk. It is the part where he reminds his audience they will all face obstacles but to never let fear hold them back. Jeff says, "As long as you know why you are in the business you are in, you will ultimately succeed." He is right. Far too often I have started marathons with fellow runners who entered the race on a dare or because they thought they will do only one marathon so that they can boast about that. These people frequently fail to finish when the going gets tough because their motivation is not compelling enough.

We endure endlessly when we have a reason and purpose. Henry Ford said, "Obstacles are those frightful things you see when you take your eyes off your goals." Christopher Columbus said, "You can never cross the ocean unless you have the courage to lose sight of the shore." To overcome adversity it is critically important to have a reason and a motive to hang in there. As an endurance athlete I know that without a proper motive it is extremely unlikely that you will be able to move forward when the going gets tough.

Maybe you are fighting for the survival of your marriage. The test of time wore both you and your spouse down. It certainly did not polish you up to shine brightly. I can predict your success of getting things back to the original ideal by asking this one question: *Do both partners have a why?*

In other words, do both believe the marriage is worth fighting for? If you can say yes, I am glad. If you cannot say yes, do not give up yet. Overcoming adversities against all odds—some use the term *miracles*—has occurred in the past, and it can happen again.

Maybe you are dealing with bad news from the doctor who called you back after a recent routine visit. The only part of this fateful meeting you remember is the first few words: "You have cancer." The rest of what was said is all foggy and hangs over you like gray, grim clouds in the dead of a long winter. Your shock temporarily destroys your memory.

Do you have a why? Why do you want to live longer and beat this cancer? Your kids need you still. Do it for them. Stay positive. Remind yourself that some cancer survivors literally used the power of mind over matter. See yourself as an overcomer. Use the power of visualization. Focus on solutions more than problems. Use words not to describe what you are going *through* but to describe where you are going *to*—the victory lane, on top of a mountain where the air is fresh and views are wonderful. Only motives based on firm foundations will enable you to survive stormy seasons.

Do You Really, Really Believe You Can?

One of my favorite scripture is, "According to your faith it will be done for you." (Matthew 9:29 NKJV) I often meditate on those words. Ten simple words, yet those words are powerful enough to change your whole perspective completely. Your trajectory transforms once you become aware of the profound truth in these words.

> **According to your faith it will be done for you.**
> **—Jesus Christ (Matthew 9:29 NKJV)**

I read somewhere that Dr. Norman Vincent Peale wrote his influential book *The Power of Positive Thinking*, first published in 1952, by hand. At some point Dr. Peale decided it was not good enough, and he literally threw the manuscript in a trash can. If it was not for his wife, Ruth Stafford Peale, who went back and dusted it off, this classic book, which almost on every page reminds us that the level of our belief matters a great deal, may have never been published. *The Power of Positive Thinking* has sold over thirty million copies. Unlike many other best sellers it has never gone out of print. It continues to remind me, daily, of the power of our beliefs.

I am not saying that if you have enough faith you will be able to win the gold medal at the hundred-meter sprint at the next Olympic Games when you are fifty-five years old. That would be a fantasy. What I am saying is that over and over I have seen firsthand how people with a strong belief always overcome their adversities in one way or another. It works for them. It has the potential to work for you. Go ahead and try it. What do you have to lose?

You might say, "I don't believe in all this nonsense." Maybe so. But remember that Henry Ford said, "If you believe you can or believe you cannot you are right both times." And the Buddha said, "All that we are arises with our thoughts. With our thoughts we create the world." Our thoughts are seeds, and the seeds we water the most grow the best.

One Step at a Time

Christopher Reeve once said, "A hero is an ordinary individual who finds the strength to persevere and endure in spite of overwhelming obstacles." During a flight to a medical meeting I read an article that illustrates this truth. The article was about a fascinating female athlete who runs a minimum of eighty miles per week. She does it with a positive attitude. She is as consistent as a metronome. The article went on to explain how she has done this for years, never making any excuses. What I have not told you yet is that she runs all these miles with one leg that is her own and one that is a prosthetic. She does it all exactly in the same way most people succeed … one step at a time.

She could have easily seen her handicap as a chain keeping her locked to her inevitable destiny. As the popular *Eagles* song "Already Gone" reminds us, so often we think we are in chains and forget that we have the keys. To me, this runner had the keys in her head. She used her positive attitude to help her run toward her real destiny.

I do not know what adversity you may be facing right now. But I know this: if you are an ordinary individual who finds the strength to persevere, *one step at a time*, it makes you a hero. Your odds of moving forward are so much better when you decide to take the first step and then continue along the path, one step at a time.

The Soft Spot Is There … Find It!

I read about two men who met in an office tower high above the streets of Manhattan. One man was getting despondent. He was close to quitting. His friend changed all that by saying, "Every problem has a soft spot. Just keep on keeping on until you find it."

I found that to be true with a recent frustration in my clinic. We were encouraged to switch to a new server for our electronic health records. At first it was a nightmare. Many a day I left the office exhausted, doing my best to keep my eyes open until I could at least flop onto a couch at home. Our staff got sick from being under relentless pressures. Our learning curve was steep.

I was prepared for the challenge based on feedback I'd received from another clinic that had gone through this pain a few months earlier. I also had a reason for persisting: it was a more efficient product that not only benefitted patients but also the staff and my colleagues. I reminded myself that positive thoughts would carry a higher energy that would last longer and help me endure without measure. If I did not believe there was a light at the end of the tunnel, I was doomed to further times of ongoing stress. I took it one day at a time—small steps. It was just like running my marathons one mile at a time, not worrying about mile twenty when I first had to get through mile ten and a steep hill that would test my resilience.

Today the system is serving me and my patients very well. I am still learning new tricks once in a while. Even so, I use it like a remote control. There are many, many buttons on the average remote control, but people rarely use all those buttons; we use what works for us and match it with our own style or habits.

If It is Not Written Down, You May Fail

The benefit of writing down your adversity is that you can see it on one page. It also forces you to define what it is and what steps could help you grow from your struggle.

I learned this method from my days as a Dale Carnegie instructor. This training was founded in 1912. For the past one hundred years it has passed the test of time. It continues to deliver results; millions of people have improved themselves all over the planet by taking this simple and timeless training.

Here is a powerful method Dale Carnegie, the master communicator, taught me and millions of others. When faced with a problem, ask these four questions, and write the answers down somewhere on paper where you can see them frequently.

1. What is the problem?
2. What is the cause of the problem?
3. What are some solutions?
4. What is the best solution?

In my journal I often use my fountain pen to write down these four questions. In my clinic I write down these questions for patients to consider. My fountain pen often catches young patients' eyes. My little patients, especially the ones under ten years old, often say things like, "That's a nice pen. How do you use it?" Or they ask their parents, "What kind of a pen is that?" They are curious, as kids tend to be.

I encourage you to write out the answers to these four key questions when faced with an adversity. Look at your responses often. Allow your subconscious mind, which never sleeps, to dissect through your adversity, layer by layer. Peel away the layers of your adversity like you do the layers of an onion.

Again and Again … Day In and Day Out

Consistency is *the* key.

In the fall of 2012 something happened in my life that empowers me to speak about consistency. I marked a milestone of one thousand consecutive days of running. I ran every day for at least a mile or more. I never ran less than fifteen to twenty minutes, and I totaled between eight and ten hours per week.

I am often asked about my motive, which is to use my exercise time as a tool for personal growth. I meditate; I de-stress; I set fresh goals; I am recreated. This growth is not just for selfish reasons but also for those whom I come into contact with as a father, doctor, writer, and part-time journalist. Running has not only sharpened my mind and created many of the ideas in this book but has also given me strength to handle disappointments.

One such disappointment took place on a certain Friday the thirteenth while I was in Phoenix. After completing my usual daily run I noticed a message on my phone. It was from the *Globe and Mail*, a nationally distributed Canadian newspaper. They had decided to replace me after I'd served them for two years, writing excellent weekly columns on children's health. They said that they were happy with my work. They thanked me for helping them launch a successful project but then informed me it was time for them to dismiss me.

By running daily, I was able to manage my disappointment, and as I said earlier, this unexpected disappointment did pass. The tide shifted. The rejection became my protection because it enabled me to write about topics that resonated better with my own style. All is well now. I have written a book instead of writing for a newspaper that dictated my topics. I have more time to train for another Boston Marathon. It means more to me when other media outlets, who still regularly ask me to contribute, such as *CTV Morning Live* and the *Calgary Herald*, tell me, "Great job as always." It is an honor I deeply appreciate. Their loyalty over many years means a lot to me.

When I consistently exercise, I am also able to be more consistent in other areas of my life. Consistency cultivates the inner strength needed to persevere under pressure. In my case running marathons has made me more resilient.

Job and Patience

In the Bible, Job was a very wealthy individual. Then one calamity after another befell Job. All within the span of a few hours he lost family, wealth, property, and other things he valued deeply. His wife encouraged him to curse God. He sat on a dunghill and scratched at his itchy and inflamed boils. He remained patient and said, "Even if God slays me shall I still believe and trust in Him." (Job 13:15 NIV)

Today there is indeed a dermatological condition called Job syndrome. We also have the expression "To have the patience of Job and the wisdom of Solomon."

Let's fast-forward to the end of Job's story. God blessed Job by giving him twice as much as he had before; in the end Job had more than the beginning. He lived an amazing life, dying at the age of 140.

I often witness huge debates as to whether he actually existed and as to why he suffered so much. That is for theologians to sort out, but even though they debate their theology, they all agree on one thing: Job was patient through all his adversity.

Patience pays off when facing adversity. Stay unperturbed. Do not fret. And when friends come to you trying to help you with their sincere ideas, make sure that these friends are real friends. We need friends on our side who are patient with our struggles. We need them to be in our corner.

Who Is in Your Corner?

I have had the honor to work as a medical doctor since 1979. After all these years certain patterns stand out. I am specifically thinking of what I have seen when adversity strikes families and they come and see me for help.

I have noticed what I call *the three Fs*: friends, faith, and family. Some patients value friends more; others rely on their faith; some rely on all three, and when they do, they seem to have an *extra* sense of resilience.

> **When dealing with disappointments always rely on the three Fs: friends, family, and faith.**

One of the most impressive studies I've ever encountered explored the powerful impact our supporters have on us. Researchers were able to get a group of nuns in Minnesota to agree to sacrifice their brains for research posthumously. What the pathologist found was a huge surprise. Although many of the nuns died at a ripe old age, few exhibited clinical findings of Alzheimer's disease, though their brain histologies were completely typical of the cellular changes seen in dementia and Alzheimer's. How could this be so?

The most plausible explanation was that these ladies for many years felt the love and support of their close friends. They exercised together and stayed in good physical shape. Their faith was precious to them. They often laughed together, cried together, and had each other's backs when adversity struck. Their community was like family—perhaps that is why they are called *sisters*.

When we look at our future and the predictions of various pundits, it is easy to see that all of us will need more resilience to cope with future adversities—the world is going through unprecedented turmoil. Volatility has become the new norm. In the future our true friends will become even more essential if we are to cope with what lies ahead.

Scientists have studied how vital relationships generate resilience. For example, institutes like the Stockholm Resilience Center generate resources respected by millions globally. This center now attracts attention in a manner never experienced before. There are new political orders on the horizon, and economic patterns all around the world are that of government debt never seen before. How we will move forward and not get discouraged will depend on how much we water our resilience seeds.

As a pediatrician I am particularly interested in how parents play a role in helping children and teens become more resilient. I believe we owe it to the next generation to share with them ideas that will help them in their journeys of moving forward. We need to be in their corner.

Adversity Often Comes Unexpectedly, but You Are Carried

In my own life I did not know what a massive curve ball was waiting for me at Thanksgiving 2011. I was to be polished and pruned like never before. I had to make a simple choice when the road forked at just before midnight in the physical realm as well as in my mind.

My wife was driving at the time because I needed some time to meditate and regain the energy I'd spent navigating us through all the tricky passes of the Canadian Rockies. It was late at night, and the kids were asleep in the back. I was feeling grateful for my family and for having completed my seventy-eighth marathon a few days before. Since we were almost home, I decided to check my e-mail on my smartphone. I read an e-mail I shall never forget ...

My dad had e-mailed me explaining that he'd lost a lot of weight. He went on to describe how the doctors had discovered diabetes. But that, sadly, was not the end of the problem. The words "and then they gave me the sad news that I have Stage IV cancer of the pancreas" hit me like a baseball bat over the head. I paused. Then I read it again to make sure I'd read it right.

I quietly told my wife the news. My voice was weak and my heart heavy. It was a new affliction to hit our family, a capital *A* Adversity. My first response was to pray intensely about this bad news. Prayers do not always lead us to the perfect place we perceive for ourselves, but sincere, in-depth prayers bring peace.

> **The words "and then they gave me the sad news that I have Stage IV cancer of the pancreas" hit me like a baseball bat over the head. I paused. Then I read it again to make sure I'd read it right.**

In the days following, I was impressed by the number of my friends and acquaintances who, when told about our family's adversity, all independently said the same thing: "I am so sorry about your dad. I shall pray for you." Even people who had never before talked about prayer uttered those words. Independently the same pattern emerged.

A few weeks later I found myself in a plane over Africa, on my way to spend time with my father in Cape Town. I did not know what to expect. I tried to encourage myself that dark night at thirty-five thousand feet, wide awake while the majority of passengers around me were fast asleep. I reminded myself of a quote attributed to Mildred White Struven that had caught my eye a few days prior to this trip: "A clay pot sitting in the sun will always be a clay pot. It has to go through the white heat of the furnace to become porcelain." We grow into our full potential when we are exposed to the heat of adversity.

I also reminded myself of the famous poem "Footprints." In the poem a person is in trouble but believes God is walking beside him all the way. When he looks back at the sand, two pairs of footprints are proof of that. Except at one point there is only one set of footprints, raising the question of why he suffered all by himself at that point. God answers that at that point it was not the man's footprints but God's—God carried him through the toughest times in his life.

My frail dad met me at the airport with a weak but grateful smile. When I hugged him, I felt only skin and bones. His breathing was labored. Pancreatic cancer was doing its best to devour this dear man I loved so much. That afternoon we visited until he was too tired to sit up. Shortly after sunset he went to rest.

Many thoughts swirled through my mind that evening. It was one thing to *read* about adversity. It was something completely different to find myself in the midst of this brand new chapter in my life. I suddenly arrived at a place of inner knowing. I was reminded of the famous words "Life is difficult," penned at the beginning of the book *The Road Less Traveled*. I now understood, with both my mind and heart, the real meaning of those three words.

The next day I discovered what I refer to now as the *BEST method*. BEST stand for **b**elieve, **e**xpect, **s**ay, and **t**hink positive.

Here is how it helped me. Less than two weeks after I arrived in Africa, my dad died around two o'clock one Wednesday afternoon. I was there when it happened. I shall never forget what I felt when he took his last breath. At that point he'd already closed his eyes for the last time an hour before. I looked down at his wristwatch, which kept on ticking. It reminded me that time never stands still. We all will die one day, but until then we must live life on purpose. My dad had made peace with God before his spirit left his broken body. My dad was a great example to me.

In the midst of a storm, I sensed the unconditional love of a creator. From this adversity flowed an inner knowing that all will be well. This experience will forever be a precious moment in my life.

My dad taught me the BEST method by the way he lived his life. At the time I did not see it. Through an inner work of cleansing and healing I grew through this sudden reminder that divine appointments always appear on time, as they should, and for a greater purpose. I *believe* that he was the best father anyone could have asked for, I *expect* to meet him again in heaven just as he met me at the airport (with a smile on his face), I *spoke* words of hope and encouragement into his life every day I spent in his hospital room, and I *think* of him often.

In fact, as I type these words, I am sitting in a condominium he bought in the Canadian Rockies. Almost mystically, I sense him looking down on me. Even after his death, he continues to inspire and guide me. The best way I can honor his legacy is to do what he did so well. He was unselfish, considerate, compassionate, energetic, kind, and nonjudgmental, and he never gave up except toward the end when the intense, relentless pain of pancreatic cancer caused him to pray that he would die soon. Angels ministered to him in the very end, and his prayer was answered.

In this same condo my dad bought, I read a quote by Chuck Palahniuk: "We all die. The goal is not to live forever; the goal is to create something that will." My dad taught me much in the spiritual realm. He did it without words, through his deeds.

He also left a physical legacy by allowing us to enjoy our visits to one of the most serene spots on this planet. Many weekends we go to the condominium he willed to my family in order to escape the pressures of caring for patients and refuel our tanks. By doing so, I have been able to refuel my mind, body, and spirit in order to serve others better and fulfill my destiny.

> **We all die. The goal is not to live forever; the goal is to create something that will.**
> **—Chuck Palahniuk**

I am sharing with you the BEST method—one that was created during my time of adversity in Africa. It is something I believe will work for you. But only if *you* work at it when you face whatever unexpected adversity may lie ahead of you.

Check your *beliefs* daily. *Expect* the best, but leave the final outcome to a higher power. Observe what you *say* as it relates to overcoming adversity. Affirm you are a winner, even when it may look as though the opposite will happen. Declare that you have what it takes. And finally, by daily intentions, *think* positively. By deliberately applying the BEST method, you will attract the resources you need to handle hardships. You are sowing the seeds of success, which will manifest provided you persist.

Dr. Norman Vincent Peale refers to this ability we have to overcome as *the persistence principle*. This principle states that there is positive energy *already* inside of us, and we allow it to flow out of us when adversity tests our resilience. It will allow us to move forward, and in doing so, you will help others do the same. Moving forward is not selfish. It is all about our resilience inspiring others to develop their own abilities to overcome life's inevitable adversities. Imagine how far all of us will move forward collectively if we inspire one another to become more resilient.

Adversities allow us to become more aware of what really matters. They awaken us. Introspection teaches us compassion, but only if we keep our hearts open. To move forward we also need to check our ability to maintain what energizes us the most. In the next chapter I shall share how we can enhance our energy.

Action Steps

1. *Know that you will face adversity at some point in time.* It is inevitable. Life is impermanent. Nobody is immune. Therefore it makes sense to be prepared for the inevitable. Have a list of how you were able to manage your adversity in the past. Review this list often, and *apply* your past lessons.

2. *Make sure you have your priorities in life written down in capital letters and where you can see and affirm them at least once a day— ideally every day.* Consider frequently the motive that fuels your functioning. Priorities must be crystal clear because if they are not, you may just give up too soon. We *all* have a destiny and purpose. Don't forget your purpose when troubles try to derail you.

3. *Make sure that you have a mentor or coach, somebody who can help you grow and who can help you defeat your adversity.* One of my mentors reminded me recently that pearls come from oysters

that are constantly irritated; the bigger the irritation, the more beautiful the pearl.

4. *Don't do what most losers do and focus on the problem more than the solution.* Remember the words of a wise person who stated that winners focus on where they are going *to*, while losers focus on what they are going *through*.

5. *Never give up trying again.* I shall never forget my seventieth marathon where I ran thirty seconds too slow to qualify for the Boston Marathon. That was about a second per mile too slow. I decided to research why I'd missed my goal by such a slim margin. The persistence principle has kept me going in my quest to cross the Boston Marathon finish line once again.

6. *Have an anchor that is fully dependable.* Life at times is simply too hard to manage alone, and friends or family will fail at some point. I have experienced the faithfulness of my creator both in good and bad times. The spirit always has the last word, even though it may not seem to be so at the time. Remain open to the power of positive faith next time you face troubles. Stay connected to your source. Alignment with our creator means that we are in harmony with creation.

7. *Use the BEST method often, especially when it comes to dealing with bad news.* Personally I check carefully what I *believe* about the problem; I always *expect* to overcome in the end; I carefully watch the words I use to describe the situation, make sure that I *say* what is positive only, and *think* thoughts that are uplifting, optimistic, and power-packed. By using the BEST technique I plant and water these sacred seeds consistently. Always monitor your inner dialogue.

8. *Your motive is to improve yourself in order to serve the world.* You have been born for a purpose. Your life matters. Allow whatever you do or say to be motivated *above all else* by loving kindness.

CHAPTER 2

ENERGY

The key to focus is not time management,
but energy management.
—Rick Warren

In order to move forward, overcome setbacks, and encourage those we come into daily contact with, we need energy. It is hard to give what you do not have. In this chapter I will discuss practical ways to ensure we vitalize ourselves consistently when life is doing its best to pull us in various directions all at once. Distractions dilute our energy, especially when we get tired in our minds before we get tired in our bodies.

My first questions to you are very simple: What plans do you have that allow you to increase *and* maintain your energy? Are you mindful of *all* the energy zappers in your life? These are vital questions all of us must ask ourselves. Simple as the questions may be, they can make a huge difference in determining your successes or failures. You may have *all kinds* of skills, potential, and goals, but without energy you may be like a top-of-the-line luxury car without gas. Energy is like fuel—without it you will get nowhere. The key is indeed energy management, perhaps more important than time management.

In the medical environment good health is marked by what clinicians call *homeostasis*, a state of balance. Eastern philosophy calls it yin and yang. When talking to my patients, I use the analogy of a stool with three legs. The three legs represent the mental, physical, and spiritual. Ideally, all three must be in balance. Since our minds are powerful in creating reality, let's start with looking at how we generate mental energy.

Mental Energy

A lack of mental energy seems to be all too common these days. One of the most common complaints I get from my patients is "Doctor, I am so tired. I lack energy. Can we run a few tests please to see what is wrong with me?" By the time my usual history and exam are completed I have the diagnosis pretty much wrapped up. The root of the fatigue is mostly mental and *far* less frequently due to disease or pathology. One of my mentors, Dr. Norman Vincent Peale, says that more often we get tired in our minds before we get tired in our bodies.

We do not need some wonder drug to give us more energy. What we need is a strong, positive mental attitude, an attitude that will provide us with the vitality to prevail, not just when things go our way but also when we find ourselves in the middle of a long, dark night unexpectedly going through the shock of a sudden loss.

In order to maintain a high level of mental energy, we need to become aware of the things that erode our energy deposits. These are things that have enslaved us, also called *memes* by evolutionary psychologists. These negatives block the signals we get from our souls. Negative energy derails us from our true destinies. These energy thieves operate like pickpockets by distracting us and stealing energy when we are most complacent.

If you are not in a place of peace and lack energy right now, chances are you are giving your attention to what ancient mystics called the *five poisons.* These poisons allow our energy to leak steadily, one moment at a time. The leak is insidious, similar to a slow leak from a screw embedded in a vehicle's tire. The screw allows small amounts of air to escape overnight, and by morning we are surprised by a flat tire.

The following are the five poisons:

- ignorance—lacking a deeper awareness of what will bring us peace
- egoism—allowing our egos to be in charge, which tell us how unfair life is, how we should compete harder, and how we are not measuring up when we compare ourselves to others

- attachment—not wanting relationships, health, finances, and job opportunities to end
- aversion—meditating and worrying about the things we do not want, such as cancer, rejection, or maybe a new career or a new location
- fear of death---a fear often associated with a sense of us having no control over the inevitable.

One way to change the situation is to meditate more often. If we say we are too busy to meditate, then we are too busy. We end up being stuck in a rut; inertia keeps us in the same spot. As Alexis Carrel, a French surgeon and biologist, observed, "Life leaps like a geyser for those who drill through the rock of inertia." I encourage you to drill through the inertia resulting from nonmeditation; consider instead a rhythm of daily meditation.

When we take action by meditating on what energizes us, we get unstuck. We move forward. Meditate on what nourishes your soul. Silence is a daily gift you give yourself. I often think of meditation as a massage of the mind. It is a daily habit that can help you realize your life's calling. Whenever I see homes and malls under renovation, I cannot help but wonder why we are so focused on physical renewal yet neglect the renovation of our minds through meditation.

Meditate on something your favorite author wrote, or meditate on a holy book that speaks to you. Pick one verse that stirs your soul. Personally I dwell on "Be still and know that I AM God," "I am kept in perfect peace if I keep my mind fixed on God," "In quietness and in confidence lie my strength," or simply the two words "Fear not." Change both your intention and your attention. That which you focus on expands, so focus on light—not darkness.

Be Fully Present

So much has been written on being fully present. Some simply refer to this state as *mindfulness*. The emotions we experience are determined by our thoughts. Discontentment—the inability to simply be fully in the present and failure to accept things as they are—can drain our energy. Our presence is elsewhere.

I read a story in high school that illustrates how we all are guilty at times of wanting to be elsewhere. Instead of being in the present and enjoying what we experience right now, we yearn to be in another's shoes. This can drain our energy. In the story there were two men: one was in a train and the other in a tent next to the railway line. From the train where the man was enjoying a delicious meal, he saw the other person enjoying a meal in his tent by candlelight. He thought that it may be more fun than his usual meal in the usual dining car. Meanwhile the man in the tent thought the person in the dining car had a better deal.

To this day, this wonderful story comes to mind when I remind myself that my energy comes from contentment with where I am—as opposed to constantly wanting to be somewhere else. Spending mental energy on the wish to be elsewhere can lead to fatigue, especially if we fail to take the time to become quiet and meditate on the topic of being fully present in the now.

Be Grateful

Research shows that people who make it a daily habit to pause and be grateful enjoy more energy. Gratitude has been called the forgotten factor in happiness. Grateful people are more active physically, they relate well to others, they are more generous, they worry less, and they enjoy a greater sense of vitality. The words *think* and *thank* have the same root. When we meditate (think) on the long list of things we could be grateful for, taking the time to actually name them one by one, we place ourselves on a perfect path to experiencing more energy.

Dreams and Desires

There are moments when we lack mental energy, even after hours of meditation, simply because we delay our dreams and desires. Fear may hold us back. We wait until we are ready. Successful people start before they are ready. They listen to their passions, and by living in advance and behaving as if their dreams are already so they move forward with profound vitality.

I made this discovery when I applied the wisdom of Dr. Wayne Dyer who, when working on a book, designs the cover first. He then places this cover by his sacred writing space. It keeps his passion for the book alive. The cover of

Moving Forward was a reality before the pages of this book manifested. By keeping copies of this book's cover on my desks at home and at the office long before the book was completed, I was able to keep the dream alive.

Control by Design

One major leak of mental energy is wasting energy on that which we cannot control. The Serenity Prayer reminds us to live one day at a time, enjoy one moment at a time, accept hardships as the pathway to peace, take the world as it is and not as we would have it, trust that all will be well, surrender to the will of God, and accept the things we cannot change while also having the courage to change the things we can. We are to hope for the wisdom to teach us the difference between what we can control and what we absolutely cannot control, even if we think we can.

In the end, it is only our minds we can control; 90 percent of what happens to us depends on how we choose to control our thoughts. Our minds establish the reality in which we will live. We must cultivate the habit of daily looking into our perceptions, making sure we do not waste energy on things we cannot control, like the weather. How we perceive and frame life determines our attitudes. Sometimes we can look at old pictures, and simply by changing the frame, we are able to change the picture. One can say we are in the reframing business!

One such person who is wise in focusing mainly on what she *can* control is Louise Hay, the founder of Hay House. Hay is eighty-seven years old at the time of writing this book. She illustrates the power of having an energetic life by writing: "As I look back and think why I feel so good at age 87, I truly believe it's because of the way I live my life. My thoughts from morning until I go to sleep at night are filled with positive affirmations. I truly believe that Life loves me and that everything I need comes to me at the right time." Not only does she focus on what she can control, but she also pays close attention to her own daily affirmations.

> **I truly believe that Life loves me and that everything I need comes to me at the right time.**
> **—Louise Hay**

Affirmations

In addition to paying attention to what we can control and what we cannot control, our words and affirmations also may contribute to how energized we feel. For example, if we go around confessing over and over "I am sick," in our subconscious mind we become victims of disease. A better alternative would be instead to say, "I am experiencing sickness." This teaches us that we are learning lessons from what we are going through. It is a more positive approach. If we affirm what we do not want to experience, we activate negative energy; instead affirm what you intend to manifest. The law of attraction, a metaphysical law, states that like attracts like. Many of those who are uncomfortable with the concept of metaphysics nevertheless talk about self-fulfilling prophecies, essentially referring to the same principle.

Relationships

So often our emotions are determined by the quality of our relationships with others and ourselves. With many of my patients I have observed that toxic relationships can be a major energy leak. Hanging on to anger, bitterness, hate, resentment, fear, unforgiveness, guilt, and jealousy comes with a high price. It can disturb our mental health, especially when these emotions accumulate over years. It drains our peace.

There are many definitions of toxic relationships. Take for example dealing with people who are manipulators. These people usually have huge egos. They believe that they must always be the sun and never a planet. In other words everything must revolve around them, and if they are not around, there is no light.

If you allow them, manipulators will control you at every opportunity. If you require their approval in order for the relationship to be at peace, then it will always be a major reason for your fatigue. You are spending energy to please others. Meanwhile you don't run your own race. You are allowing manipulators to push you off course. You are not living the life you are destined to live. Instead you please manipulators and allow them to manipulate you.

I have also observed that manipulators can be very charming. Butter cannot melt in their wholesome mouths. They make it look as if they get on well with 99 percent of other people, but with you they struggle. In essence they are saying, "I am such a nice person. I wonder what your problem is that you don't like me." Meanwhile that's just one more way for them to manipulate you into doing what they want or even at times *demand*!

Very few people enjoy conflicts and confrontation. I am one of those who try to avoid conflict. Strife opens the door wide for all kinds of troubles. Not so long ago I learned a valuable lesson. Research shows that out of all the people you will have to deal with, 25 percent will like you regardless. They will support and encourage you. They are on your side. About 50 percent can be swayed either way, to like you or dislike you.

That leaves another 25 percent of people with whom you never will get along. No matter how hard you both try, it will not work. They rub you the wrong way. They drain your energy immediately. The way they operate just does not sit well with you. You do your best, and it seems the harder you try, the worse things get. Just accept that no matter what you do it will be so. Move on. Don't allow them to drain your energy. You have an assignment to live life authentically, and it takes lots of energy to do that. So just move on. Let those nasty types be who they are. You can't change them—only God can. Forgive them. Don't be bitter toward them. Wish them well, but move on. Instead seek out those who appreciate your gifts, and work with them to help each other improve, grow, and live on purpose

> **Research shows that out of all the people you will have to deal with, 25 percent will like you regardless**

The other night I had the opportunity to watch Rick Warren, the author of *The Purpose Driven Life*, discuss the roots of conflict in relationships. Here is his list of common causes of conflict:

- self-centeredness
- stubbornness
- pride
- poor listening skills

- insensitivity to needs of others; inability to see things from another's perspective
- not speaking the truth in love; being abrasive instead
- attacking and blaming the other person
- using insults
- assuming you know the motives for the other person's decisions
- destroying the dignity of the other person.

The Bible teaches us to avoid strife at all costs. There may be many good reasons to observe this warning, but one thing is for sure: conflicts drain our energy, and that may be one of the top reasons to avoid it.

In Dale Carnegie's classic book *How to Win Friends and Influence People*, he mentions first and foremost the three things that can ruin a relationship: criticisms, condemnations, and complaints. I completely agree with Dale Carnegie that we need to avoid condemning others, but is there perhaps a practical and easy-to-remember alternative?

I discovered such a choice when a mentor told me that we should treat others as if it's *their* last day. When we do that, we will be less selfish, more compassionate, less judgmental, more encouraging, less impatient, and more understanding. In short, we will stop sweating the small stuff.

If the way we relate to others determines our energy levels, how does relating to ourselves contribute to fatigue? Diane Von Furstenberg said, "You're always with yourself, so you might as well enjoy the company." However, some of us do not enjoy our own company, because we tend to be hard on ourselves.

Being hard on oneself is far too common. We often tell ourselves we are too old and tired to try to move forward. Abraham Lincoln said, "In the end it is not the years in your life that count. It's the life in your years." It is as if some of us live lukewarm, gray, half-effort lives after a certain age. As a result there is very little life in our years. I am reminded of these people who never saw themselves as too old to make their contributions:

- Charles Darwin was fifty years old when *The Origin of Species* came out.
- Leonardo Da Vinci was fifty-one years old when he painted the Mona Lisa.
- Abraham Lincoln was fifty-two when he became president.

- Ray Kroc was fifty-three when he bought the McDonalds franchise and took it to unprecedented levels.
- Dr. Seuss was fifty-four when he wrote *The Cat in the Hat.*
- Colonel Harland Sanders was sixty-one when he started the KFC franchise.
- J. R. R. Tolkien was sixty-two when *The Lord of the Ring* books came out.
- Ronald Reagan was sixty-nine when he became president.
- Jack Lalane was seventy when, handcuffed and shackled, he towed seventy rowboats.
- Nelson Mandela was seventy-six when he became president of South Africa.

Excuses

In my work as a physician I have also observed how many patients make excuses for their unwise decisions. Instead of blaming themselves for their fatigue, they blame other factors. They seem to never move forward; they are stuck in one place, and over time, depression dilutes whatever energy they had before.

Making excuses can start at a very young age. I heard a story recently of a five-year-old boy who could not sleep. He wandered into his parents' room, and they told him to go back to his bed and count sheep. An hour later he was back and informed his parents, "Sorry to tell you, but one of the sheep I counted peed in my bed." This story, which is really a window into the soul of a child, is humorous, but it is not humorous when adults have an aversion to accepting responsibility for their own actions.

Once we stop making excuses and blaming others we can get serious about being in better control of our mental energy. Make the relationship you have with yourself a priority, and be motivated not by ego but by the words of Christ, who said, "Love your neighbor *the same way you love yourself*" (Mark 12:31;emphasis mine.) Sadly, too many have focused on the love they have for their neighbor, at the cost of forgetting how to relate well to themselves. We say bad things about ourselves we never would say to a close friend. If we did utter those negative words to our friends, they would be shocked.

Guilt and Regrets

Two of the most toxic emotional drainers are guilt and regret. It is true that we cannot unscramble eggs or have a better past. I heard a useful piece of advice not so long ago: "If the past calls, let it go to voice mail. It has nothing new to say!" I also heard a life coach tell a client to have a radical pastectomy. The only reason to look back at the past is to see how far you have come.

Alan Cohen stated that guilt was invented by the Jews and perfected by the Catholics. He also notes that babies are born guilt-free. Guilt is a habit we develop over years and years of conditioning.

Learn to manage guilt by refusing to carry more than you need to. Elizabeth Potier said, "It isn't life that weighs us down, it's the way we carry it." Leave guilt and regret along the road and move on; refuse to carry these emotions like a backpack glued to your body.

If our souls—our minds, wills, and emotions—are wisely organized, we are more productive, at peace within, and more creative. We have more to offer, and we can serve one another far better and more consistently. It is easier to be disciplined, we endure longer, and we are better equipped to manage inevitable obstacles. People like to be around us, and we live our lives more intentionally—as opposed to drifting on the surface of a lake like a dead piece of wood.

Stay patient. Be consistent. Be gentle toward yourself. You will make progress as long as you hone your mental focus. Allow these ideas to permeate *deeper each day* until they become part of who you are.

Physical Energy

When you discover ways to intentionally increase your mental energy, you are off to a good start. But as the saying goes, "Bean by bean, the bag gets filled." We move forward one step at a time, however long it may take. Another adage says, "All acorns become oak trees." It is by patiently accumulating skills that we move forward. Let us change gears now and look into the physical choices we can make to enhance our energy.

A few years ago I was in Colorado Springs, attending a conference for doctors. The topic was balancing faith, practice, and family. I could not believe what I saw: hundreds of tired doctors. These tired professionals were the same people who were supposed to tell their tired patients how to heal!

Needles to say, it concerned me deeply. I sat down, and using my fountain pen, I scribbled on a yellow legal pad a two-page list of reasons for this fatigue. I looked at that list again and again during my flight back home. I looked for a common theme and tried to spot a pattern. I could not see the answer until a few days later when I entered an alpha state during an early morning run. (Some call this state a "runner's high.")

I was running alongside a slow-flowing river. I heard the happy sounds of birds chirping away. The tempo of my strides triggered the answer: These tired doctors were mostly out of sync with their bodies; their souls were struggling to remain positive, and their spirits were disconnected from their creator's best plan for them. Some of them were not doing things that made their hearts sing. Perhaps they could not say, "This is who I came here to be."

These fatigued physicians allowed themselves to become too busy. The predictable excuses surfaced: too busy to exercise, not enough energy to spend on self-care, too many things to get through before it was time to sleep. I understand that those who need excuses use them. The healers themselves were suffering from what I call the *lukewarm disease*. This disease occurs when we hardly exist; we simply survive. We do not thrive with zest, and we allow our vitality to slip away.

I observed that many failed to exercise daily. In addition, many of their wounds were self-inflicted. These doctors did what most of us do: fail to exercise daily, go to bed too late, eat too many junk foods, worry more than needed, overcommit, allow limited time to have fun with friends, and lack a consistent routine that provides daily revitalization.

I maintain top-ten lists that I share with my patients who want to increase their energy by eating healthier, exercising more consistently, and sleeping soundly. These lists, intentionally limited to only ten points per list, are based on my observations accumulated over close to four decades as a clinician. Given the current upward trend of obesity, I consider food to be the first starting point.

Food

It has been said that there are only four food groups in North America: McDonald's, Burger King, Wendy's, and Pizza Hut. I tell patients in my pediatric weight clinic that there are two ways to approach fast food outlets: go there no more than twice a month, and when visiting, reduce portions or order the least unhealthy foods. Digesting junk foods requires more energy.

I have a passion for teaching healthy eating in the two clinics I work in. If eating like a Greek means eating more plant-based foods, doctors have thus far been unsuccessful at changing the facts: only 2 percent of the population eat the recommended daily intake of produce, despite all the government campaigns and miles of bookshelves filled with ideas on how to eat more vegetables and fruits.

We do not need more information. We need to help people experience more energy as a result of clean eating. For some families, especially those who live farther away from the equator where the winters last long, one solution is to consume fruit and vegetable supplements. Like Dr. William Sears, I too recommend Juice Plus, the most researched fruit-and-vegetable supplement at the time of this writing. It is natural as opposed to man-made.

Not only do I pay close attention to my fruit-and-vegetable intake in order to fuel my body for its daily runs and the quest to reach one hundred marathons by age sixty, but I also *visualize* these natural foods going to work at a cellular level. I do what a friend, Dr. Mitra Ray, once said: "Picture your cells *radiating* health."

Here is a top-ten nutrition list to get your cells to radiate:

1. Eat like a Greek. I am talking about the Mediterranean diet, a meal plan that, unlike many other diets, has passed the test of time. The majority of other diets fail because they are too complicated or boring over time. The Mediterranean diet is the ideal spot of nutrition. It works because it is balanced. It is not extreme. It has been said that the first thing we do on a diet is cheat. Because the Mediterranean diet is so balanced, cheating is less likely.

2. It is not one issue of low carbohydrates or low fats. It is not either-or—both matter. So eat only healthy fats and healthy carbohydrates. Some say it is all due to fats, and others say it is all about sugars. In fact we have no clue about nutrigenomics (how our genes determine our response to various food types). Having said that, I do encourage my patients to know more about the glycemic index and the glycemic load. I also provide them with a specific simple list of good fats and bad fats.

3. Find what eating habits work for you, and then be consistent with this plan. There is no such thing as one size fits all. Science at best has a rudimentary grasp of how our genes determine our individual response to various foods.

4. Keep the portions smaller, especially around suppertime. An example of how an ideal plate should look can be found at www. choosemyplate.gov.

5. You can never, never eat too many fruits and vegetables. *Never.* Dr. Joel Fuhrman in his best seller *Eat to Live* suggests two pounds of raw vegetables daily.

6. Be wise with your alcohol intake. Avoid it or limit it to occasional consumption instead of regular use. In addition, drink more water or dilute sweet juices with water if you find plain water too boring.

7. Always combine protein and fiber with your carbohydrates.

8. Chew your food twice as long as you do now. Eat slowly as if you are sitting peacefully and in no hurry, under an umbrella on a sunny, calm day overlooking the deep blue Mediterranean Sea.

9. When you make your own food, you have the most control. Have fun eating out or ordering in, but aim to make your own food far more often than eating food prepared by others.

10. The only vitamin I recommend is vitamin D. A diet rich in fruits and vegetables provides us with natural sources of vitamins— except vitamin D. For adults, the reasonable dose is 1,000–2,000 IU per day, and for children, it's between 400–800 IU per day.

> **When asked what the ideal meal plan is, my answer is brief: eat like a Greek.**

Exercise

When it comes time to get active, I am reminded of the story of a man who was sitting by a fireplace. The fire was dying down. He asked the fire for more heat, and the fire answered, "Give me more wood." The man responded, "No, first give me some heat; then I will give you more wood."

I wonder if that is not the situation at times in our own lives. We feel too tired to exercise. If we were to go outside for a minor workout despite feeling tired, we would return with more energy. The solution may be to act as if you have more energy. Even if you are tired, the mere act of feeling enthusiastic will send a message to your subconscious being. *Assume* the feeling of vitality even before you work out. Then ensure you choose the right environment for your physical activities.

There are two places that energize me consistently every time I run there: Central Park in New York City and the Golden Gate Bridge in San Francisco. I saw a headline not so long ago that read, "Hollywood's Love for the Golden Gate Bridge." It's a love I share, and one of my favorite moments on that bridge was a few years ago when I was participating in the San Francisco Marathon. We were heading south from stunning Sausalito. To my left side, in the far distance, I could clearly see the San Francisco skyline. Suddenly a few feet ahead of me I noticed a fellow runner on his knees, proposing to a female runner. There was a special energy in the air when she said "Yes!"

When we tune in to the right frequency of energy—similar to tuning in to the right radio frequency—we experience joy, love, and peace. For many of us nature is where we experience an inner stirring. Nature becomes a sacred place where we observe the existence of a force much bigger than ourselves. We refer to a stunning sunrise by the ocean as "awesome." Some of us remember to be in awe at that moment. We experience the intelligence behind it all. It allows us a sense of peace that permeates deep into every cell in our body.

I am blessed to live close to a body of water, and I always pause during my marathon training by a sundial overlooking the lake and the snow-covered Rockies to the west. These words on the sundial remind me to soak up my environment and allow it to move my soul in the right direction: "May the joy of nature inspire your direction in life."

Personally, I experience a surge in energy when I am in awe of my own body's ability to run marathons. I am also energized when I consider the force that created and sustains my body. This higher power inspires me to feel my union with creation. Yoga practitioners become aware of an oneness, a union, when they mindfully execute their various postures each day. The word *yoga* means union.

However, I appreciate that not all of us enjoy exercise that much, even after trying the above suggestions. To illustrate, I attended a pediatric meeting in Florida when the United States was shifting their health-care delivery. As part of the Affordable Care Act some places of employment provided pedometers to their employees. The idea was to help them get active and then track the number of steps. This sounded like a good idea, until it was discovered that some employees sat on their sofas and shook their pedometers to make it look as if they were taking steps!

Some use humor to describe their lukewarm approach to exercise. Jack Bennie said, "Give me golf clubs, fresh air and a beautiful partner, and you can keep the clubs and the fresh air." And Zig Ziglar explained that before he started to exercise regularly, his idea of exercise was to fill the bathtub, pull the plug, and fight the current!

> **Give me golf clubs, fresh air and a beautiful partner, and you can keep the clubs and the fresh air.**
>
> **—Jack Bennie**

Here is a top-ten list of exercise suggestions to increase or maintain your energy:

1. Find the kind of activity you enjoy the most, and do it at least four to five times a week for thirty minutes.
2. To avoid boredom, develop a mix of aerobics, flexibility, and strength-building activities.
3. As you get older, do more weight training to counteract the body's natural trajectory of muscle loss. This will pay off especially in the senior years when falls are a common reason for hospitalizations and subsequent disabilities.

4. Get a personal trainer. Your physiology is constantly in flux. These trainers know what the ideal, customized plan should look like for each stage you experience. As someone once remarked, "Do not go to the hardware store to look for milk." I say, "To know what it's like to have a baby, ask a woman, not a man." In other words use an experienced trainer who walks the talk, one whose lips and legs move in the same direction!

5. Only compete with yourself; run your own race at your own pace. Your body is unique; treat it as such, and stop looking at what talents others may have. It is good to have examples to inspire you, but do not imitate others—be original. A common reason for discouragement is competing obsessively.

6. Genetically some of us are simply 100 percent averse to exercise. Do not use that as an excuse. It may require more effort. You may be envious of those who are wired so that they are able to exercise effortlessly. Forget about them, and instead, honor your uniqueness.

7. When you are tired, intentionally exercise at minimal effort. If it gives you more energy, be grateful; if it makes you tired, then accept that, and try again another time. With persistence you will eventually discover what works best for you.

8. Keep most of your exercise effortless. My coach Grant Molyneux's book *Effortless Exercise* does a great job of guiding an athlete to get into his or her own zone. I highly recommend it as an endurance athlete. I often use a prescription pad and Rx this great book instead of prescribing pharmaceutical Band-Aids.

9. As much as possible be active in nature. Research comparing indoor and outdoor exercise, using the same effort in both venues, has shown that those who exercised outside experienced more lowering of blood pressure.

10. Remember that motion creates emotion. I first heard this from Tony Robbins and agree 100 percent that motion creates emotion, based on running an average of 3,500 kilometers each year. Running makes me *feel* as if I am on top of the world.

Sleep

Controlling our exercise and nutrition carefully may not provide us with more energy unless we pay closer attention to how we pace ourselves by intentionally designing a resting routine.

One of the major blind spots for many of us is that we may be doing well with nutrition and exercise, but we cut corners when it comes to getting enough rest. We allow no margins of rest. Thich Nhat Hahn reminds us, "It is very important that we re-learn the art of resting and relaxing. It allows us to clear our minds, focus and find creative solutions to problems." He adds, "We humans have lost the wisdom of genuinely resting and relaxing. We worry too much. We don't allow our bodies to heal, and we don't allow our minds and hearts to heal." How many of us fail to move closer toward our goals simply because we ignore messages our bodies share with us?

Yawning is a simple message. The next time you catch yourself or someone else yawning, remember that as someone once said, "Yawning is my body's way of saying 20% battery remaining." Dale Carnegie taught us to rest before we get tired. And if you feel guilty about rest, remember that the heart spends more time in rest (diastole) than pumping (systole). Nature's rhythm can teach us something very valuable.

At bedtime as our rhythms slow down, it is wise to cultivate vital routines. Before I go to bed at night, I often remind myself of these words spoken by Victor Hugo: "When you accomplished all you can, lie down and go to sleep. God is awake." As Dr. Wayne Dyer so insightfully reminds us, regardless of our opinion of God, our fingernails grow at night even when we are fast asleep. Our creator is in control even if at times we are unaware of his love for us. We need not worry, fret or fume. I remember the story of a man who always left a chair by his bedside. When asked about this peculiar habit, he said it was to remind him that God never sleeps. Thus there was no point for both him and God to be awake at night. Instead he went to sleep soundly, allowing God to stay awake and use the chair as needed. God *always* does the night shift.

Here is my top-ten list for allowing the body to rest and recover every night:

1. Know how much sleep your body needs. Vacations are the best time to establish this. For example, go to bed when you start to feel sleepy, and wake up when you wake up. That is how you listen to your body. It is fair to assume you will require more sleep if you dramatically increase the volume and intensity of your exercise program.

2. Be very careful during the hour or so before you go to bed. Dr. Wayne Dyer, author of *Wishes Fulfilled*, makes the point clearly that the subconscious never goes to sleep. Like a computer, we can input both good and bad. Choose wisely. Do not check e-mail that may upset you before you retire for the day. Make sure that when you use the words *I am* they are followed by something positive such as *blessed, rested*, or *going to reach my goals*. It gives the subconscious positive material to work with while we sleep soundly.

3. We are all guilty of cutting corners by having an inconsistent bedtime or wake-up time. Limit the inevitable inconsistencies induced by a self-imposed jet lag.

4. Keep a dream journal. If you see a pattern, start paying attention more closely.

5. Before you buy a book on sleep or see a sleep specialist, invest in a top-quality mattress and pillow. It is also far too common to keep electronic devices close to your head at night—avoid having a cell phone by your bedside.

6. Accept the fact that as you get older your sleep patterns will change. We tend to need less sleep as we advance in age. Only get concerned if sleep patterns are getting increasingly worse.

7. Naps are a great way to recharge. If you can catnap, be grateful. Limit the duration to no more than twenty minutes. If you unable to nap, take one-minute vacations: close the door of your office, sit back, and visualize your favorite vacation spot on the planet for one minute.

8. When you cannot sleep at all, remember what Dale Carnegie says in his book *Stop Worrying and Start Living*: "The Perfect way to conquer worry is to pray."

9. Snoring may be hard on those who must try to sleep close to you, but it is harder on your health than you may realize. Get it fixed—for your sake *and* your partner's own energy.

10. Although more and more family doctors are taught about sleep medicine, the best resource is a doctor who specializes in this area. It is still an evolving science fraught with many myths.

> **Snoring may be hard on those who must try to sleep close to you, but it is harder on your health than you may realize.**

Environmental Energy

Our physical energy can be enhanced when we pay closer attention to our physical environment. There are three key areas in our environments—where we live, where we work, and where we play. We can enhance our energy by improving these environments.

Where We Live

Our homes are shelters where we wake up and where we return after trips or a long day at work. Our homes should be places of peace, joy, and comfort—oases where we can retreat, refresh, and enjoy some downtime in peace. In *The Poetics of Space* Gaston Bachelard says, "I should say the house shelters day-dreaming, the house protects the dreamer, and the house allows one to dream in peace."

My study is one of my favorite rooms in my home. I always sense a higher level of energy when I do my writing and reading there. When I write in this sacred space, time becomes meaningless. I am lost in the moment. I am fully present. Some refer to this as being in the zone, similar to a runner's high.

I keep my library in the study. This takes up too much space according to my wife. I told her what Horace Mann said: "A house without books is like a room without windows." In the end my wife may be partially correct, though. Einstein said, "Out of clutter find simplicity." Clutter can drain energy, and at one point my study *did* become somewhat cluttered. I have arranged the books better, so it now has a cleaner look, and I don't have to waste energy looking for a book when I need it. A lady once observed, "My house is not a mess. It is just that everything is on display for your viewing pleasure—like a museum." It may be a humorous way of looking at things, but in the end clutter can drain our energy.

About eighteen years after my wife and I moved into our home, we decided to renovate. Home renovations can test one's patience. Rarely do we hear about a single renovation project that was done on time and on budget! Renovations are disruptive. And yet all the chaos and inconveniences can come some good. Renovations help us to simplify. In going over stuff "stored" in the basement, I dusted off some old, useful books and long-forgotten clothes. Cleaning out closets also helped me to see the value of order and simplicity. It is energizing to eliminate clutter.

When we enter a room that is almost Zen-like in its simplicity, we can sense the higher energy level. My running coach has such a study. He also happens to be debt-free, happily married, and the father of a top student. He drives a clean car and stays active all year round. He is well organized, and rarely have I seen him tired. He is a master at keeping his home and personal life uncluttered.

Recently I read about the brain child of a New York City–based director of an advertising agency: six items or less. This project is an exercise in frugality and an effort to pare down a wardrobe. The concept is simple: wear only six items over one month. Many people who took on the challenge and found that it's really easy to do. They also discovered something else: no one noticed that they wore the same six items over one month.

> **The concept is simple: wear only six items over one month.**

A home that lets in light is a home with energy. My two favorite rooms in our home—my study and the bathroom—both face east. Doing some writing or interviews with media from my home is that much easier when, in the mornings, I can observe the sunrise and see the sun's bright rays fall on my desk.

I find doing my usual morning grooming in the sun symbolic of freshness. It is the start of a new day. That is why I appreciate a bathroom that lets the bright morning light stream in.

In addition to keeping a home uncluttered and bright, I have found fragrances to be paramount too. Medical studies tell us that there is strong link between our emotions and the olfactory system. How many times do we observe that a smell also brings back memories? For some of us, the smell of baked cookies or a dad's cologne can take us back to our childhood in an instant.

Colorful and bright flowers also add something to our sense of smell, and this simple habit can energize a home with very little effort. Even in our home away from home we can use flowers to bring natural energy in our space. When I stay at the Andrews Hotel just off Union Square in San Francisco, I notice they make it a point to leave flowers in the rooms.

I keep my clothes closet tidy. A few years ago I discovered a store just off Union Square. It sells the finest Italian clothes outside of Italy! Since those clothes fit me perfectly the first time and last longer than other garments, it is almost the only place where I shop for clothes. I do my best to consistently dress neatly, not only because I am on TV every week but also because my energy level is so much higher when I put on a nice, clean jacket that fits well and looks sharp.

Looking for more peace at home? Try using a water fountain either inside or outside the home. There is something about gentle, trickling water that brings peace and tranquility. The sound of a brook or a steady stream of water echoing in a room can set one's mind at ease after a long day at the office followed by a traffic jam on the way home.

Where We Work

If you enjoy your work, you are blessed indeed. If you hate your job, you are a slave, according to Mother Teresa, who said, "Work without love is slavery."

I was honored to serve as the president of the Community Pediatric Section of the Canadian Pediatric Society. One of the fun responsibilities was to call the recipient of the Distinguished Pediatrician Award, an award given out once a year to a community pediatrician in Canada who was nominated by his or her peers for his or her contributions as a clinician, teacher, researcher, and mentor.

I remember calling Dr. Moshe Ipp, a Toronto-based pediatrician, to inform him that he had won this award. His response will forever be stuck in my mind: "I really enjoy my work and working with families. It's a real surprise to do what you love and then get an award like this for having so much fun." I could sense from Moshe's tone that he was truly thankful to be able to help his patients each and every day he entered his busy clinic in Toronto.

I remember very clearly the day the Challenger Space Shuttle exploded soon after takeoff. One of the astronauts who perished once said he felt guilty for getting paid to do the work he so much enjoyed. It reminded me of something Confucius said: "Choose a job you love, and you will never have to work a day in your life."

I know of a minister who owns his own debt-free airplane. He uses it as tool to get him anywhere in the world. He is in such high demand as a speaker that his independence allows him to be on fire and do the things he is good at. It is always a real honor for me to hear him talk about his passion to use time wisely, to continually grow, and to help as many others as possible to grow in their faith.

This teacher is completely gray, not because of age but because of genes. He only needs a few hours of sleep, and he is always on the lookout to bless others with his zestful approach to living. He will never retire from his calling, and he admits that he fully depends on God for his energy. I learned from him that it's an interesting experience when reading the Bible to substitute *my source* every time we see the word *God*.

> **Choose a job you love, and you will never have to work a day in your life.**
>
> **—Confuciust**

In the ballroom of a fancy hotel in Orlando I heard something that has stayed with me for years. An Irish small-business owner was sharing how he had been able to grow his business so rapidly. He told the audience that if work is not fun, then it is because you are not doing it right. The same can be said about people who dislike their work. If you are in this group, then change your intent by finding a new way to re-energize yourself or finding another work situation that you can enjoy more consistently. Maybe you need to find a new occupation, change to another field, or change your attitude. The longer you wait to do that—perhaps out of fear—the harder it is going to be to live a vitalized life.

The productive American inventor Thomas Edison once said, "If we did all the things we are capable of, we would literally astound ourselves." His method of achieving success at work was simple: rest when you get tired, and work when you are rested. Despite all his hard work, he lived for many years, but he always made sure that he was in harmony with his energy levels. He was not only a genius in his inventions but also a genius at pacing himself so as to always be filled with vitality.

Few would argue that Leonardo Da Vinci, another creator, lacked energy and ideas. He followed his own advice: "Every now and then go away, have a little relaxation, for when you come back to your work your judgment will be surer; since to remain constantly at work will cause you to lose your power of judgment. Go some distance away because the work appears smaller and more of it can be taken in at a glance, and lack of harmony or proportion is more readily seen."

I once heard someone say that it is better to go from rest to work than to go from work to rest. Far too often we don't pace ourselves and need to rest. It is better to energize oneself in rest and, like Da Vinci or Edison, become more productive, being fueled by fresh energy.

Creative people raise their energy by going through three stages:

- accumulation
- translation
- dissemination

First creative people accumulate ideas and information for what they want to create. Take a book for example. Then they write it one page at a time, reminding themselves that the main purpose is to serve others, and finally they share their creativity by disseminating the book to those who may be interested and ready to benefit.

Enjoying your work not only keeps you vitalized but also may delay the aging process. The actress Sophia Loren saw creativity as a fountain of youth, saying, "There is a fountain of youth: it is your mind, your talents, the creativity you bring to your life and the lives of people you love. When you learn to tap into this source, you will truly have defeated age."

As much as we love our jobs, it is important to draw a line between work and play. It has been said that almost nobody has pictures of their office hanging on the walls of their homes. When there is an imbalance between work and play, it is as if the spokes of a wheel are not the same length, and the wheel rolls in a wobbly manner. The ride is never smooth until we establish a sound, balanced energy field. Dave Barry was correct when he said, "You should not confuse your career with your life"

Where We Play

As I write this, I am seated in the very back of a Boeing 737, heading south toward Mexico. In my family we are blessed to make heading away from the cold, dark northern climate of Canada an almost annual tradition for spring break.

Earlier, just as the plane had been pushed back, Jonathan, my son and seatmate, had pointed toward two men standing outside on the tarmac, holding up a big banner that said, "Have fun in the sun!"

Having had the privilege to grow up in a sunny environment in Africa, I am always energized when I feel sunshine on my face. Being in a bright environment brightens one's spirit, soul, and body.

A few years ago I had the opportunity to meet a yogi from India. We were guests on a local breakfast TV show where I was a regular medical contributor at that time. The yogi's topic was sunshine and how we can survive on sunshine *alone*. It was amazing to hear him explain to one of the anchors, in a calm and peaceful manner, how he was able to generate energy *only* from sitting in the sun.

Afterward I told him how being in a sunny place like Mexico energizes me. He was not surprised at all and added that walking barefoot on a beach allows one direct contact with the earth. In his opinion this direct contact allows energy to flow into our bodies. I am always aware of a higher vibrational energy when I find myself next to the ocean.

This blissful state is explained by this observation: "We are what our environment makes us and if our environment is such as to produce excellent health, beauty, joy and comfort it will reflect immediately in our lives." This has been confirmed by research showing that people who live next to the ocean find that experience invigorating. Wallace Nichols's *Blue Mind* goes into more detail, using scientific data that shows how being close to water makes us happier, healthier, and better at what we do.

> **We are what our environment makes us and if our environment is such as to produce excellent health, beauty, joy and comfort it will reflect immediately in our lives.**
>
> **—Author unknown**

In addition to oceans, mountains consistently raise my vibrational energy. Recently I was surrounded by various peaks of the Rockies. It was summer, and the doors and windows were wide open. The fragrances of flowers hung in the air. The day was coming to an end, and the setting sun touched only the tips of some peaks; other mountaintops were already covered by dark-pink shadows, created by the fading sun, making way for the full moon rising above the wide-open prairies.

I consider looking at these majestic mountains a privilege. I could stare at them for hours, simply being in the moment and marveling at their splendor. Becoming quiet and soaking up my connection with God's creation serves as a reminder that my help comes from my creator (Psalm 121:1). The great news is that nature is *free*! One does not need money to purchase many things we take for granted, such as the sun, mountains, oceans, rivers, and the moon. These things are there for our free enjoyment. They are divinely designed to increase our energy if we set aside time to appreciate them fully.

Mountains and oceans have a lot in common. They both remind us of how small we are compared to them. They are timeless reminders of a creator creating a world much bigger than we may ever know. It is safe to say these wonderful slices of nature at its best will still be there *long* after we are gone. There is a higher vibrational energy level associated with them. They have a peaceful rhythm.

Lily Tomlin noted, "For fast-acting relief, try slowing down." It is to the mountains and oceans where I go to get my own fast-acting relief … The mountains and oceans are my symbolic aircraft carrier whenever I need to come in for a landing to get refueled. They are places where I get to reset my tempo, where I have better control over my pace. Life is like running a marathon: it is all about pacing oneself wisely.

When I feel in harmony with nature, I feel a total peace. This generates a sensation that makes me affirm, "I can never get enough of this place."

> You owe it to your soul to find your own place of serenity to reset your vitality. Do not put it off until "someday."

A few years ago I was invited to a nutrition conference in Switzerland. I shall never forget my early morning run in Lausanne, a city next to Lake Geneva. That particular morning I ran by the headquarters of the International Olympic Committee on my way to the edge of a lake that reflected the mountains in its mirror-smooth surface. I can still "vacation" there in my mind to this day anytime I feel stressed or under pressure. I felt fully present in the moment on that particular morning, probably because of my natural surroundings but also because I felt one with all other human beings at that international conference.

Being in the moment fully—especially when at play or admiring nature—affects your mind, will, and emotions by infusing fresh vitality. You owe it to your soul to find your own place of serenity to reset your vitality. Do not put it off until "someday." Energize yourself by *design*, not by default. Use your place of play to uplift you.

Integrating Physical Energy

There are many other resources out there on the topic of energy and physical causes of fatigue. I am partial to the comprehensive science of functional medicine. I have seen how patients increase their energy level dramatically in months by applying the concepts contained in functional medicine. For more information on how to be whole when it comes to nutrition, sleep, and exercise, I highly recommend the Institute of Functional Medicine website to my patients: https://www.functionalmedicine.org/

Spiritual Energy

Far too often we look at physical and mental causes for fatigue, and we miss a blind spot: the spiritual aspects. These forces are powerful. They can make energy flow like a river in springtime when the snow is melting or suddenly block our energy like a plugged-up washbasin.

In the Bible, we read that we are to "guard our hearts with all diligence" because from the heart flows all the issues of life. Having energy to sustain us daily is included in the word *all*—all the issues of our lives flow from the heart. We may not always be aware of it, but we live from the inside out. Once we experience the peace of staying connected to our source and learn to trust God's timing, we experience authentic peace. We remain calm, content, tranquil, untroubled by setbacks, complete, whole, and certain of our purpose in life.

The root of spiritual energy is to be aware of your connections. Divine connections can provide a life marked by love, joy, peace, patience, kindness, goodness, gentleness, faithfulness, and self-control. To consistently live life this way requires energy. We get to decide if we have the ability to fuel ourselves or if we need the support of a higher power as our source of energy. I have observed that people who stay in sync with this provider experience what Dr. Peale refers to in one of his books as the *plus factor*. These people always grow. They move forward daily.

Religion cannot provide this higher energy. By relating to the divine, by having God as a partner, and by becoming aware of God as the ultimate source of energy, we experience fresh energy. Religion, when driven by rules and regulations, cannot change lives. Some say traditional religion is man-made. Anything man-made is finite. It is prone to corruption and hypocrisy. There are limits. Traditional thinking can pollute true spirituality. True spirituality, the kind that vitalizes us, deals with our *relationship* with a higher power and how this relationship impacts others we relate to.

Unlike ADD (attention deficit disorder), the cure for what I call spiritual deficiency disorder (SDD) often is a major crisis or loss. A dramatic shift in life raises the ultimate questions about our purpose on the planet. Life can change in an instant. What we thought we controlled suddenly swirls rapidly out of control. Our energy is gone; our pain penetrates deep into our being. Suddenly we realize we don't control all the levers. The checkers are moved by forces we cannot control. As I said before, life has taught me that we may try to understand God, but the truth is we can at best only understand this invisible force *in part*. The Bible says that God is unsearchable. It also adds that nobody knows the mind of God and that nobody understands His thoughts. So be still and surrender. Stay detached from the outcome, because you are not in full control every moment of your brief time on this planet. Do not waste energy trying to figure it all out. Instead remain connected to divine energy.

Sometimes we feel disconnected from our source. But as we wait on Him, our strength gets renewed, as Isaiah 40: 31 reminds us when it says, "But they that wait upon the Lord shall renew their strength." Marathon runners often include this scripture on the backs of their shirts. It has made the difference between quitting and getting a finisher's medal many a time for various marathoners who had their strength renewed by relying on God's energy.

I like to set the tone of each day early in the morning, ideally close to sunrise. I find that time of the day extremely symbolic for fresh starts. I use it as a time to meditate on why I was allowed to wake up yet again and to be reminded of my connection with God. It is a time when I combine my running with thought discipline, a term one of my mentors used to describe positive faith.

> **I consider the first and the last moments of our days the most important. They set the tone of what follows next.**

I like to set the tone by meditating at these keys moments, using my BEST method. I make it a habit to review the foundations of what I believe about divine energy. For example, I believe that divine joy provides strength. The joy of being connected to God is my strength. The fact that I am still alive means there is a purpose for me to fulfill in the moments ahead.

I then visualize what I am expecting from the day and write down my three highest intentions and expectations. It has been said we generally get what we expect (the law of attraction).

As I continue my meditation, I do my best to control one of the most influential muscles in my body—the tongue. It may be small, but like a small match it can set a forest on fire. What we say about ourselves and the situations we may encounter sets the tone each day. Affirmations are powerful.

Lastly, I remind myself that positive thinking is a habit and that to overcome bad habits we need to replace them with another activity—it takes the same amount of energy to think positively as it takes to think negatively. One might as well take a chance with the positive choices!

Following this routine of being mindful of what I *can* control, I always reflect on what it means to my energy level when I become detached from the outcome and leave my future in the capable hands of a higher intelligence. This intelligence makes the grass grow, the sun rise, my heart beat. It is a loving force. Even if there are times when I choose to edge God out, I am still loved.

Early in the mornings, before sunrise, when I meditate in my study, I often hear birds sing outside. This always reminds me of the quote "A bird does not sing because it has an answer; it sings because it has a song." We may not have all the answers, but each one of us needs energy to express our songs. I cannot think of a better way than to ensure fine-tuned balance of the mind, body, and spirit.

Recently during one of my morning runs I spotted a beautiful red rose. On top of this rose were a few dewdrops reflecting the sparkling rays of a bright morning sun. I had to stop and smell it. At that very moment I thought, *It would be very difficult for even a genius to make a rose like this from scratch.*

As I continued my run and felt the warm sunshine on my face, my energy level soared as I meditated on the words spoken by another runner in the movie *Chariots of Fire*: "When I run I feel God's pleasure in me."

I experienced an almost overwhelming sense of awe for the creator who made the rose, ensures that the sun keeps on shining, directs my paths, and is defined by one word: love.

When you are tired, why not check your own beliefs carefully, expect things to get better, speak words of faith and optimism, and think about possibilities instead of thoughts that deal with toxic emotions such as hate, resentment, bitterness, guilt, fear, anger, or jealousy. Allow the wisdom of the creator to uplift you daily. This energy will always support you. It is rooted only in love. The key to moving forward is indeed energy management.

So far we have been reminded that adversity teaches us our best lessons. We have seen that energy management is as important as time management—or perhaps at times even *more* important than time management. In the next chapter we will look deeper into the benefits of developing consistent, daily disciplines that provide us with the power to endure, persevere, and move forward.

Action Steps

1. *Make the time to pause and sit down with a pen and paper.* Reflect on what activities, decisions, and events energize you the most. It is important to remember that this applies to *you*. Personalize it. It may be useful to do this once a week, for example on a Sunday night, which often is the transition between a relaxing weekend and the start of a busy week ahead.

2. *As you go over the list of things that energize you the most, note which ones are mental, physical, and spiritual.* Make sure there is balance between these three areas. If I learned one thing from the Taoist philosophy other than living life with simplicity, humility, and compassion, then it is to be balanced.

3. *Be sure the list is useful and achievable.* If the list is not customized or if it is unrealistic, the chances that you can translate it into consistent habits are diminished. For example, you may not be able to go to a sunny spot every few months, but how about deliberately

getting outside on a sunny day, perhaps during your lunch hour, to soak in the sun for a few minutes?

4. *Keep the list short, and pick one or two things only under each category of mental, physical, and spiritual.* Be sure you can realistically do each activity consistently over the next three weeks. We know from research done at Harvard that those who write down their visions, plans, and goals are far more likely to achieve them.

5. *Put that list where you will see it every day for the next twenty-one days.* It may be where you brush your teeth, put on your makeup, or shave, or it may be on your fridge or in your daily planner or diary. If you use an electronic planner, be sure to back it up often.

6. *Be accountable to yourself.* Although it may be wise to have an accountability partner to whom you report regularly, this may not be practical for some. Remind yourself that ultimately it is up to you alone to be consistent and disciplined. Remove excuses. Remember you will either have results or excuses. Therefore make an appointment with yourself once a week. Review what worked for you and what caused you to lack consistency.

7. *Be grateful for all the things that are right in your life, for the things that give you energy each day, for new insights, for fresh wisdom, and for an increased level of consistent living.* Count all the positives first before you allow a negative default setting to kick in. A grateful attitude causes vitality to flow freely. Dr. Daniel Amen calls these negative default settings ANTs (automatic negative thinking)

8. *Remember the ripple effect.* Your energy can energize those you associate with. Be infectious, and raise the vibrational energy of others.

9. *If you find your purpose in life, you will have far more energy.* Learn from the hero firefighters who survived the sorrow of 9/11 by taking up running in Central Park in the middle of the night to honor their fallen friends. Be enthused fully. Not having a specific greater purpose decreases our sense of significance. It is an enormous cause for energy leaks.

10. *Enthusiasm and energy flow together.* Remember the word *Entheos* (root word of *enthusiasm*) means "God inside of you." If you are open-minded and want more energy, consider allowing God to fill

you with His energy, and always be thankful for that. Whatever your image of God may be and whatever name you choose to describe God, know that this higher intelligence will always be available as long as you remain open to divine energy.

Chapter 3

Discipline

Rule your mind or it will rule you.
—Horace

Sowing the seeds of daily discipline can make a dynamic difference as we try to tackle life's challenges and overcome them.

I have been inspired by the wisdom of Alan Cohen, who wrote, "Everything has a cost and a payoff. Make sure your payoff is worth the cost." How we move forward hinges on the commitments we make daily; consider the cost of these commitments, and remind yourself that your discipline determines your destiny.

Nelson Mandela observed that running taught him valuable lessons. Mandela claimed, "In cross-country competitions, training counted more than intrinsic ability, and I could compensate for a lack of natural aptitude with diligence and discipline. I applied this in everything I did."

Discipline requires constant commitment. Some of us have conditioned ourselves to link any perception of discipline with Spartan living. Discipline is the steering wheel of life. I see it also as moments of enlightenment. We move forward when we discover which of our daily habits support our souls and defeat our discouragement.

Discipline does not have to be hard. It simply requires a constant commitment to stay open to what equips us the best. In living a life of service to God, others, and ourselves, we should seek constant growth. When we do that, we move away from all our shoulds, such as "I should exercise more, and I should eat healthier." A better approach is to ask,

"What would I have to do to follow my heart in such a way that I will develop the skills to do what I am called to do?"

The Dalai Lama, in *The Art of Happiness*, expresses his understanding of a disciplined mind this way: "Whether our action is wholesome or unwholesome depends on whether that action or deed arises from a disciplined or undisciplined state of mind. It is felt that a disciplined mind leads to happiness and an undisciplined mind leads to suffering, and in fact it is said that bringing about discipline within one's mind is the essence of the Buddha's teaching."

> **It is felt that a disciplined mind leads to happiness and an undisciplined mind leads to suffering. Bringing about discipline within one's mind is the essence of the Buddha's teaching.**
> **—Dalai Lama**

I believe that daily discipline is always preceded by mindfulness. We take the time, *intentionally*, to consider the day ahead. Daily meditation is about getting quiet and becoming receptive to the moment. We get into the habit of interrupting our rabbit minds, with endless thoughts running randomly through our minds, often creating negative emotions and draining our energy. Some have likened feelings to waves. We can't stop them from coming, but we can choose which ones to surf. What we meditate upon determines our feelings. We get to choose wisely when we discipline our mind.

Recently I was inspired by Davidji, author of *Secrets of Meditation*, to become quiet and reflect on my own daily disciplines.

As a result I have committed myself to remain disciplined in ten areas that are important to me. I often review this list in what some call fractional moments, the times we wait in lines or get stuck in traffic. My own top-ten list includes these daily disciplines:

1. Always make loving kindness the top priority; nothing replaces this from being priority number one.
2. Check my thoughts carefully, and reject any negative imaginations as soon as possible. Deliberately and immediately replace worry

(negative imaging or meditating on messes) with a positive, higher-energy thought.

3. Always remain open to learning and growing more and more.
4. Take care of the body, and honor it as the temple containing the spirit.
5. Ensure I associate with the best mentors and role models.
6. Meditate at key moments, early mornings, and close to bedtime.
7. Cultivate an attitude of being grateful, and take nothing for granted.
8. Live on purpose, by honoring my chosen calling.
9. Commit to that which serves me the best, and do it with passion and enthusiasm.
10. Be consistent. Keeping my priority lists close by has now become a consistent habit I've cultivated—as consistent as my daily running since December 2009.

Loving Kindness

This past year I met a man, not in person, but because of his insightful writings. In retrospect it was not a coincidence. Robert Holden arrived on my radar screen at the *exact* time when I discovered that positive thinking, strong faith, and success all become meaningless without love. Robert, in turn, was inspired by his mentor, Tom Carpenter. This relationship led to the creation of *Loveability*, an insightful and inspiring book on the topic of love being the foundation of all our decisions.

The theme of *Loveability* is very simple but profoundly and eternally true: every issue in life either succeeds or fails based on the presence or absence of love. A well-known psychiatrist, Dr. Smiley Blanton, affiliated with the Marble Collegiate Church located on Fifth Avenue in New York City, expressed the same truth many decades ago: "Love is the answer to all human ills."

Love is the answer to all human ills.
—Dr. Smiley Blanton

When we choose to prioritize the daily discipline of growing in love, we are set free from the slavery of living an ego-dominant life. David Foster Wallace confirms this with this insight: "The really important kind of freedom involves attention, and awareness, and discipline, and effort, and being able truly to care about other people and to sacrifice for them, over and over, in myriad petty little unsexy ways, every day."

Making loving kindness a top priority when we are in a leadership position is only possible if one follows the advice of Lao Tzu, who said, "If you wish to be out front, then act as if you were behind." Always stay humble and compassionate, and keep your truth simple.

As important as it is to love others, we sometimes forget to be gentle with ourselves. When we respect and honor the way the creator designed us, we become aware that our skills were given to us. We did not earn them as a result of some stellar effort. Those skills are to be shared. We are conduits. We should respect ourselves and yet refuse to allow the ego to drive our decisions.

Some of us fail to move forward because of fear. But love, which always drives out fear like light drives out darkness, never fails. With love we experience a peaceful knowing that our disciplined living does not make us better than others, but rather allows us to live out our purpose, motivated by love. Loving-kindness begins with an awakening inside. Then it flows to those close to us and beyond. Our way of living cause ripples. We move forward, motivated by a healthy, sincere, authentic love.

When I think of why it is important to make the discipline of love a daily habit, these words come to mind: "What goes around comes around. Work like you don't need the money. Love like you've never been hurt. Dance like nobody's watching. Sing like nobody's listening. Live like its Heaven on Earth."

> **If you wish to be out front, then act as if you were behind.**
>
> **—Lao Tzu**

Thoughts

The Roman emperor Marcus Aurelius said that the world we live in is determined by our thoughts. Ralph Waldo Emerson wrote that a man is what he thinks about all day long. Plato said our thoughts can make or break us. William Wordsworth explained that our thoughts can create either a heaven or a hell. The Bible reminds us that as we think, so are we. It also adds that we can be transformed by the renewing of our minds. For centuries we've seen the same pattern of observations—what we think upon expands. Everything that now exists was once a thought.

Because perceptions are more important than reality, the discipline of cultivating the right thoughts can never be overstated. To say that the mind—what we believe and think—determines our future is an understatement. Instead it ought to be written in bold letters. When we carefully consider our thoughts, we protect or energy; we can endure without limits and position ourselves to move forward consistently.

I have been inspired by Dr. Joe Dispenza, DC, author of *Breaking the Habit of Being Yourself,* to "never let a thought slip by my awareness that I didn't want to experience." Doing this is not easy considering how many thoughts we entertain in a day.

In James Altucher's book *The Power of No* he offers a compelling solution to being bombarded daily by over sixty thousand thoughts: ask, "Is the thought useful or not?" Doing this has frequently helped me to focus on that simple question. Do it consistently and you will waste less energy. Your use of useless thoughts will decrease. Your higher energy level will allow you to move forward. You will get closer to allowing your convictions to serve you and others better.

> **Is the thought useful or not?**
> **—James Altucher**

In scriptures we are told to cast down every imagination and bring every thought captive to the obedience of love. Worry and negative thinking are nothing more than the habitual practice, done daily, of meditating on imaginations. We can see and speak the negative before it manifests. Yet we seem to struggle with doing the opposite—thinking and speaking positively.

It takes energy to think negative thoughts. We all want to have more energy, so why waste it on visualizing the negative when the same energy can be used to think positive thoughts? What is there to lose after all?

I carry *Thought Conditioners* by Dr. Norman Vincent Peale in my briefcase or symbolically keep it in my jacket pocket that covers my heart. In this booklet Dr. Peale writes commentaries on key verses from scripture.

One of those verses has become a mantra for me: "Peace I give to you. My peace I give to you. Not as the world gives do I give. Let not your heart be troubled; neither let it be afraid." (John 14:27 NKJV)

Dr. Peale's commentary on this verse is insightful:

> Without a deep inner state of quietness, one becomes prey to tension, worry and ill health. A song, a sunset; moonlight, the sea washing on a sandy shore, these administer a healing balm. But they lack power to penetrate the inner recesses of the soul.
>
> A profound depth therapy is required to attain healing quietness. A habitual repetition of this one text will, in time, permeate your personality with a complete sense of peace.
>
> When tense or restless sit quietly and allow these words to pass unhindered through your thoughts. Conceive of them as spreading a healing balm throughout your mind.

I believe some thoughts recur for a reason. For example thoughts about what we can control, what makes us happy, why we are here on this planet, how to be authentic, why we suffer, and how we may serve help us to discipline ourselves in such a way that we find our true purpose. Obviously for each of us the answers to these thoughts may vary, but this is how I consider these important thoughts when I set time aside to reflect each day:

- *Control what you can*, let go of what you cannot control, and wish for wisdom to know the difference. Various spiritual traditions all end up saying the same thing in the end: "Let it go. Surrender.

Allow God to work. Be led by the spirit. The universe is unfolding as it should. The Tao does nothing but leaves nothing undone."

- Aim to be *unconditionally happy*. Sakyong Mipham refers to this thought in his national best seller *Turning the Mind into an Ally* as being at "the mercy of your moods." Too often we allow our moods to be doing the navigation. Talking about navigation, I shall never forget reading a chapter on unconditional happiness in *The Untethered Soul* while flying between Orlando and Denver one afternoon. While the plane was making a gradual turn to the north, toward Denver, after heading toward the west for the longest time, I experienced a quantum moment: be unconditionally happy even if it is difficult because we are not so inclined.

- Discipline your mind and heart to become more *authentic and true to your purpose.*

- Since *suffering is inevitable*, what resources have we developed to always move forward?

- History teaches us that those motivated to serve by using their talents in areas that resonate with their spirit end up with more energy. A doctor friend calls it a "helper's high." Think about all your skills, and ask, *"How may I serve?"* Remember that we desire energy not just for ourselves but to serve others.

Our thoughts determine our emotions, feelings, and attitudes. By changing our thoughts we have the potential to change ourselves and move forward. Guard those thoughts carefully. Look at thoughts as seeds being watered daily. The seeds you water the most are the ones that will grow the most. And unlike reaching the top of Mount Everest, positive thinking is achievable by all people.

Have an Open Mind

Since I was a teenager, personal growth has always been a discipline I've honored. It continues to serve me well on a daily basis. If I had to live my life all over again, I would again value the advantages of staying open to personal growth each and every day, because we may get old in our bodies but we get to choose if we get old in our minds.

Being open-minded allows us to grow. I have told my friends I believe in being open- minded but not to the extent that my brain falls out. Discernment matters a great deal.

One of the reasons it is important to be open to growth at all times is so we can reach our destiny and move forward on purpose. George Bernard Shaw said that how we see the world begins with us: "Better keep yourself clean and bright; you are the window through which you must see the world." To have results our minds should be kept clean and disciplined.

I first recorded many of the ideas in this book with my favorite fountain pen. I record my personal growth in my journals—similar to those who take photographs to record trips or special functions. Once every few weeks I know it's time for the fountain pen to be flushed out. This improves its optimal flow—it glides over the paper once I do this. And so it is with our minds; we need to flush them out in order to make room for personal growth. In addition, our minds can become like suitcases filled to capacity; in order to put in a new item we need to take something out first. We make room for growth when we do that.

Our minds tend to get complacent and stuck in deep ruts, conditioned by our daily routines that have become monotonous—but only if we allow them to get that way. In *Turning the Mind into an Ally* Sakyong Mipham refers to this state as "the dark age." There is no need to be limited to this dark age. What is far, far more exciting is to apply the discipline of daily personal growth. It is never too late to develop this delightful discipline.

> **Our minds tend to get comfortable and stuck in ruts, conditioned by our daily routines.**

Growth by intent allows us to truly say that we may not be perfect but that today we are better than we used to be. We understand life when we look back and learn the lessons God placed in our paths. But even so, life must be lived forward. We are all under construction, works in progress. Moving forward is a project that is never finished. It's a journey. It takes discipline to look at a crowded schedule and to slow down and think about what we are thinking about and to stay open to learning new insights.

A Course in Miracles reminds us to always live to our full potential. By staying open-minded we allow what is already inside of us to develop further. The influential *Course in Miracles* states, "Who would attempt to fly with the tiny wings of a sparrow when the mighty power of an eagle has been given him?"

Take Care of Your Body

I have had the honor to run in a few Boston Marathons. The race requires fast times to qualify and thus be allowed to line up at the iconic start in Hopington. Training for this race takes daily discipline. It sounds like a painful process, but the benefits taught me much. I became more aware of the discipline of self-care—closely monitoring one's sleep, nutrition, and exercise. This allowed me to reach the finish line and enjoy *every* step taken over 26.2 miles.

We live in a benevolent universe, but if we fail to do our part in terms of taking good care of our physical bodies, then even God, the source, will allow us the freedom to make poor choices that may shorten our time to fulfill our true callings.

I find hospitals depressing places because too many people are there because they did not take good care of their bodies. According to Dr. David Katz, a well-respected Yale physician, 80 percent of strokes, diabetes cases, myocardial infarctions, and cancer diagnoses can be reduced by doing four simple things: exercising, eating healthy, avoiding obesity, and not smoking. Dr. Katz's book *Disease Proof* enlightens us on how our genetic expressions are determined by our lifestyle choices.

George Sheehan wrote, "Everyone is an athlete. The only difference is that some are in training and others are not." My daily running routine involves a minimum of at least twenty to thirty minutes, and once a week I run for three or four hours. I never take this for granted, assuming good health. Since December 2009 I have been blessed in such a way that I have never missed a day of running.

One of those regular days of running stands out. Recently there had been a run on the edges of the city where I live—at the airport, but on a runway of all places! Calgary, at the time of the launch of this book, has one of the longest runways in North America. A few days before the runway was opened, a limited number of runners were allowed to enter a race of about ten kilometers (the length of the runway from one end to the other is close to five kilometers). The announcer at the start encouraged the runners to enjoy the freedom of this historical run, because the next time they would be on the runway, they would either be in a plane or arrested for trespassing! Although the focus that day was on a special event, a side effect was that over a thousand runners were taking care of their bodies.

When we exercise, it is important to breathe wisely. As an athlete I have studied the importance of breathing correctly. The other night I was paging through a fitness magazine when the headline "Improve Your Fitness 22,000 Times a Day" caught my eye. The piece went on to describe how breathing through the nostrils increases the body's capacity to absorb oxygen. When we are at rest, breathing mindfully helps us maintain our energy and thus our ability to be consistently disciplined. When we become mindful, it's wise to imagine our lungs filling from the bottom up.

In my clinic some patients admit to being too busy to take care of their bodies. They often ask me about the use of vitamins to "fill a gap." As a physician I am always keen to learn more about the role of vitamins as a way to take good care of my body. The only vitamins I recommend are vitamin D if one lives far away from the equator and vitamin B12 after the age of fifty, when our bodies become inefficient at absorbing vitamin B12 from natural sources. Recently I discovered another way of looking at vitamins when I read in *Success* magazine, "Always Remember to take your Vitamins: Take your Vitamin A for **Action**, Vitamin B for **Belief**, Vitamin C for **Confidence**, Vitamin D for **Discipline**, and Vitamin E for **Enthusiasm**!!"

If there is only one thing I've learned from having trained and completed almost one hundred marathons, it is that one must never quit. Obviously the ideal is to run all 26.2 miles, but just as in life itself, there comes moments when we are obliged to walk. It is indeed second best. It is not what we had in mind when the event started. Yet one walks. One moves forward anyhow.

That is really one of the key messages of this book—always move forward. Keep going. Always grow. Never allow setbacks to strand you. Never allow adversities to bring your life to a screeching halt. Do not get trapped in the same place or quit in despair.

> **Everyone is an athlete. The only difference is that some are in training and others are not.**
> —George Sheehan

Learn from Your Teachers

One morning when I opened my Facebook page, a photo John Tesch had posted immediately caught my eye. It showed a bench overlooking the ocean, and the caption read, "If you could sit on this bench and spend one hour with anyone from the past or future, who would that be?" In my mind I scrolled through all the important teachers in my life: Jesus of Nazareth, my parents, Lao Tzu, Dr. Peale, Dale Carnegie, Dr. Kenneth Cooper, Alan Cohen, Dr. Wayne Dyer, Dr. Len Zoeteman, Ray Matheson, and Rick Warren. We are indeed blessed when we have teachers who help us to stay disciplined and on purpose on our journeys. Many of the teachers I mentioned are well known, but recently a complete stranger taught me a valuable lesson.

I was in Houston at a popular coffee outlet. The service was rather slow at this store, but in retrospect, I suppose it was to teach me a lesson. I had ten minutes to observe a lady intently listening to her friend. Not once did this amazing listener say anything, not once did she look at her mobile phone. Her body language said it all: "I am here to pay attention to every word you share with me at this moment."

Perhaps she had read the piece in *The Huffington Post* that elaborated on the five skills of good listeners. The article stated this about good listeners: "They give special attention to the one speaking, they listen without being judgmental or reacting too soon, they discern where the speaker is coming from, they interrupt sparingly, and they respond with understanding." This lady exhibited all five consistently throughout the ten minutes I observed her while I waited to be served.

I have determined that every situation and event can become my teacher. I admit it's a daily discipline to not judge others and events instead of simple asking, "What is it that I am asked to learn here?" Whatever discipline I am blessed with today is a manifestation of various teachers I encountered just at the right time. All have one thing in common: they synchronistically showed up when I, the student, was ready. The timing of the divine is always perfect. It has allowed me to store up wisdom as a squirrel stores nuts for later use.

Not so long ago during my morning meditations, I read a book that suddenly became my teacher—just at a time when I needed to learn the value of these great disciplines:

> mindfulness—being in the now totally; being in the flow fully

> peacefulness—an undisturbed, stupendous, sensational serenity

> cheerfulness—being filled with joy; to the overflow

> compassion—caring for all and respecting all; honoring creation

> nonjudgment—not judging others; treating ourselves gently

> humility—admitting we do not know it all

> simplicity—the deep desire for order and energy

It is one thing to want to learn from others, but ultimately lessons learned and not applied are missed opportunities. Following the input of lessons, ensure you move forward by applying them. There should be an output after an input. A disciplined mind will allow us to accomplish this.

Morning and Evening Meditation

Through meditation we raise our level of awareness. Someone used the analogy that meditation is that which cleans a dirty window so that we become aware of the moon hanging high in the sky, a moon that was already there but had not been visible because of the dirty window.

By meditating daily we water the seeds that raise our awareness level. Life coaches often explain meditation by using the acronym SODA: we stop, we observe, we stay detached as a neutral witness, and we arrive at a fresh awareness. This new spiritual upgrade is like moving from the back of a crowded plane to first class in the front. We have more space, more freedom, and more insights, which leads to even more meditation. It's a personal discipline that also benefits those we serve and support.

I am getting better at cultivating a habit of setting a few minutes aside each day—early in the morning and just before bedtime—to think and plan, to be grateful, to get quiet, and to consider my calling for that season and time. The exciting part of meditation is that one can do it anywhere and anytime. Mindfulness does not depend on having a pillow to sit on in a room dimly lit by one candle.

I often wonder what would happen if more of us contemplated how we spend our time—what if more of us enlarged our motivation to meditate and became mindful, not just to benefit ourselves but also to benefit others? As we race through our lives, what are we missing?

I shared the above with a friend in the media who used to anchor a popular morning TV show. Many years later when I visited with him at a fund-raising function, he still remembered a time when I told him that what we do before we sleep and as soon as we wake up are the most powerful few minutes of the day. Whenever I see him, he reminds me of how meaningful that routine has become to him.

Being mindful at key moments in the twenty-four-hour cycle serves us in our purpose of moving forward. Mindfulness helps us develop an inner peace with God, our source, and it delivers a deep sense of who we are. Some who intentionally meditate experience a strong, compelling urge to serve others. We thus fulfill our calling. It has been said that we were created for one purpose: to become an expression of God's real nature, which is perfect love.

Deepak Chopra pointed out another benefit of daily meditation when he said, "Just as light brightens darkness, discovering inner fulfillment can eliminate any disorder or discomfort. This is truly the key to creating balance and harmony in everything you do." When we are whole, in harmony, and in balance, we are well able to move forward.

In my study I keep Davidji's book *Secrets of Mediation: A Practical Guide to Inner Peace and Personal Transformation* not on the shelf but on my desk. This book indeed is the manifestation of an author who continues to help millions tap into what Dr. David Simon refers to in the foreword of *Secrets of Meditation* as "a daily bath of the mind."

> **Just as light brightens darkness, discovering inner fulfillment can eliminate any disorder or discomfort. This is truly the key to creating balance and harmony in everything you do.**
>
> **—Deepak Chopra**

In quietness and confidence lies our strength. Make it a daily discipline to become quiet; confidently expect to experience the strength needed to move forward. This may explain Carl Jung's view of deep meditation: "Those inner states were so fantastically beautiful that by comparison this world appeared downright ridiculous."

When a musician asked the Buddha how he should meditate, the Buddha asked, "How do you tune the strings of your guitar?" The musician responded, "Not too tight and not too loose, so it makes the right sounds." The wise Buddha responded, "Similarly you should hold your mind in meditation." This takes practice, but cultivating it allows this daily discipline to deliver a delight that energizes us.

Someone made the point that meditation routines serve both us and others. In one of his writings Sakyong Mipham stated, "With the mind as our ally and this code of enlightened behavior, it is our duty and joy to serve others." I thus consider meditation to be one of the most unselfish disciplines we can follow.

Take Nothing for Granted

Not so long ago I went for a long run in Boston while there for a meeting with the American Academy of Pediatrics. My hotel happened to be close to the Boston Marathon finish line, the site where bombs went off in 2013 and where many lives were changed unexpectedly and in an instant.

I decided to stop my run when I came close to the finish line as a way to honor those who faced that fateful day so bravely. This spot has become sacred soil to me and others. (In Washington, DC, at the Vietnam War Memorial running is not allowed as a sign of respect for the departed.)

Whenever I lace up my running shoes, I have a ritual of honoring that moment when I am able and healthy to set out for yet another run. I never take this opportunity for granted. I always see it as a brand-new run. I shall never forget the day of the Boston bombings. I was in Ottawa. It was windy, rainy, and cold. The mere fact that both my legs were healthy made me grateful as I left the comfort of my hotel and jogged for one hour in frigid, pouring rain. For an hour I meditated on the fact that that there are dozens of others who would love to just go for a walk but are unable. Here I was, free to run in the rain.

When I run in the Rockies, breathing in fresh mountain air and seeing the sparkling morning dew, I remember an early morning run in New Deli a decade ago. It was the only time in my life when I had chest pains during a run—not because of heart troubles but due to pollution in the air. Though my motto is that treadmills are for hamsters, I gladly ran indoors the remainder of my time in India.

I also had a powerful moment to be grateful not so long ago when my wife joined me for a short but blissful run. It was the first time she was allowed to run after her recovery from a potentially fatal heart condition (ventricular fibrillation). She now has a pacemaker and also a defibrillator, which is supposed to shock her heart back into a normal rhythm. Both of us remember this time of togetherness—the first milestone run since her surgery. We never have taken any subsequent runs for granted. And when I listen to her breathing at night, I offer a prayer of thanks.

Time magazine did an interview with one of the astronauts working for an extended time on the International Space Station. When asked,

"What do you miss the most up there?" he unequivocally responded, "My daily warm showers."

> **Never take your daily, warm showers for granted.**

A few years ago, soon after Thanksgiving, I got a brilliant idea while walking from my parked car to my clinic. I determined to make the walk from the car to my place of service a walk of thanksgiving. It's a walk I do almost daily, so the habit of taking nothing for granted is well established on my priority list of daily disciplines. A thankful heart is one of the greatest virtues we can cultivate, and as much as Thanksgiving is a special season set aside just to focus on gratitude, we can all do better at cultivating thankful hearts on a daily basis. It takes consistent discipline to count what is right before we count what is wrong, to count the flowers in a garden before we count the fallen leaves.

In his book *Happiness is a Serious Problem*, Dennis Prager reminds us that Judaism has a blessing for going to the bathroom: "Blessed are You God, Who created man in wisdom and created within him numerous orifices and spaces. It is known and revealed before You that if one of them should open when it should close or one of them should close when it should open, it would be impossible for us to exist. Blessed are You God Who heals all mankind and does wonders."

Since we all have to use the bathroom at least once a day, why not use that activity as a reminder to be grateful?

There are thousands of seconds in one day; I encourage you to set aside a few seconds to express your own particular gratitude. Consider closing this book right now, and pause in a place where there will be no distractions. Focus on making a list of *at least* ten things that you are grateful for.

Ponder Your Purpose

Daily meditation and stillness help set priorities that serve us and others on our journeys forward. I have observed that the happiest people are the ones who are content with their purpose on this planet. They are content with their characters, contributions, and careers. When we discover that the most important things in life are not material possessions, our priorities shift, and our discipline grows.

To illustrate, I once read about a teacher who used objects to teach the students about the importance of setting wise priorities. The teacher filled an empty jar with billiard balls. The teacher asked the students if the jar was completely filled, and they agreed it was. But the teacher was smart and then added something else—little pieces of chipped rocks, which easily found their way between the billiard balls. There was even extra space left for sand grains.

The point was dynamic enough to leave a visual impression on the students: if the billiard balls represent our top priorities and the pieces of rock the lesser priorities and the sand the least important priorities, then it makes sense to not fill the jar first with the sand but rather the billiard balls.

When we decide on our top priorities it is wise to have a list of nonnegotiables. I often meditate on my own list, and the top three areas always involve some element of reducing stress related to faith, fitness, or family. When it comes to stress management, I've simplified it to what I call my *3M approach*: music, movement, and meditation. Hardly a single day passes that I am not intentional at harnessing the power of those three habits to energize me and help me stay focused and disciplined, regardless of how I feel that day.

We all at times wonder about our purpose. One of my favorite truths from Psalms says that unless God builds the house, we build in vain. Unless we consult with our creator, asking for enlightenment about our purpose, we labor in vain. I have heard it said that one way to make God laugh is to tell Him about your plans. One of my morning priorities is to consult with the spirit of truth regarding my purpose for that day, to get input, and to listen to intuition—that still, small voice inside.

Every choice we make as we endeavor to move forward brings a return on investment. It is my goal to partner with a higher intelligence as often as possible, and this discipline has helped me in the simple daily goal of living on purpose and of bringing more light wherever I may be. Instead of living from the perspective of "give me," we grow more when we prioritize the higher energy of "make me." When we make this our purpose, our growth becomes an adventure.

Commitment

We all have been consistent in some ways, but are we consistently committed to be disciplined in the areas that matter the most? It is a constant struggle to know what we must say yes to and what we have to say no to. Zig Ziglar said, "I have to say *no* to the good so I can say *yes* to the best."

> **I have to say no to the good so I can say yes to the best.**
> **—Zig Ziglar**

We have read all kinds of books to help us stay on track. Unlike the pilot who goes off the flight path but then quickly corrects the drift, many of us can admit there is room to be more consistent in living a disciplined life, if we are to move forward.

I like to keep things simple, practical, and useful. So here is the only question you will ever have to ask yourself when considering your own self-discipline: What do I want the most, more than anything else?

My point is really simple. Do you want to be at a healthy weight, or do you desire fatty, processed, chemical-laden, fake foods more? What do you say yes to consistently? What are you committed to? Do you want to sit and watch TV all night more than you want to take a fifteen-minute walk that will allow you to live longer? And besides, why does it have to be either-or? Do the exercise *first*, and then relax watching nonviolent, nonexcessive TV. Do you want to have an affair—according to Proverbs a foolish way of living—and risk your marriage? Or do you desire the stability of being fully in harmony and committed to your spouse?

Writing a book takes more discipline than I expected. And yet I knew I wanted to get this message out. I always had a dream and a desire to write, but it was when my excitement about the project changed that procrastination melted away. Maybe you too have a message you want to radiate. Are you committed to your message? Our passion for the message gives us the discipline that directs us toward our destiny. We get better at redeeming the time and utilizing the gift of today more completely.

When it comes to a daily review of our commitments, I am reminded of an article I read in a newspaper about Charles Gilkey, a blogger. Gilkey describes on his site www.productiveflourishing.com his method of staying focused. He calls it the 10/15 split. You spend ten minutes at the start of the day checking out what must be done and fifteen minutes at the end of the day checking what happened, reviewing, and looking ahead.

Some key questions to ask are, What did you accomplish? What things did not get done today? and What one thing are you going to start on right now?

Obviously this takes a consistent commitment to discipline, but as Steven Covey remarked, "To achieve goals you've never achieved before, you need to start doing things you've never done before."

> **To overcome the challenges of life, consistency is critically important, balance is essential, energy is crucial, our associations matter, our faith must be strong, and love has to be the ultimate motive.**

Agatha Christie said something inspiring: "To get ahead, get started." It is simple but also profound. Once we actually add action to our desires to improve and grow, it often is not as hard as we initially thought it to be. Remember that blowing up a balloon is always the hardest at the start. Once we reach a critical point, it gets much easier. Similarly the Apollo spacecraft burned off the equivalent of an Olympic swimming pool of fuel every twenty seconds just to lift off, but after a while its trajectory took less effort.

Once I heard Jim Rohn said: "What is easy to do is also easy *not* to do." It explains well why we do the things we do when we know the things we know. It also explains why every new year, many TV stations have guests on their morning shows explaining why the majority of us fail in our quest of reaching our New Year's resolutions.

In the end it all comes down to what you want more, what you are the most committed to. The investment required to make a marriage good or the pain of divorce? The pain of regret may end up being worse than the discipline it took to make your spouse a priority. A nice meal at a popular restaurant or the battle of the bulge that just got harder because you cut corners? Working out and reaping the benefits or having your life cut short by death or disease? Benjamin Franklin pointed out that there are indeed all kinds of pleasurable experiences that aim to distract us from our personal disciplines, yet he cautioned us, "Do not bite at the bait of pleasure till you know there is no hook beneath it."

For things to change you have to change, and it all begins with commitment to that which we value the most. Thomas Huxley said, "Perhaps the most valuable result of all education is the ability to make yourself do the thing you have to do, whether you like it or not."

In his book *Taming the Tiger Within*, Thich Nhat Hanh said that if we get angry easily, it may be because the seed of anger in us has been watered frequently over many years, and unfortunately we have allowed it or even encouraged it to be watered. To be in control of our emotions we need a daily commitment to mindfulness.

Consistency

Lack of consistent commitment ultimately leads to failure. In order to move forward we must be consistently disciplined. It has been said that consistency is the foundation upon which all success is built. If the foundation is strong, you are far more likely to fulfill your destiny.

My friend Joni Dowd, who lives in Texas, is one of the most consistent people I know. Joni lives a disciplined life simply because she follows the rhythms of her heart and makes daily focus on consistency her priority.

> **If we get angry easily, it may be because the seed of anger in us has been watered frequently over many years, and unfortunately we have allowed it or even encouraged it to be watered.**
> **---Thich Nhat Hanh**

Joni recently shared with me one of her methods to be consistent on a daily basis. Here is Joni's "The Ten Scrolls":

1. I will make and keep commitments.
2. I will greet this day with love in my heart.
3. I will persist until I succeed.
4. I am nature's greatest miracle.
5. I will live this day as if is my last.
6. I am the master of my emotions.
7. I will laugh at the world.
8. I will multiply my value a hundredfold.
9. I will act now.
10. I will seek guidance.

Montaigne wrote these words to remind us of the importance of daily goals: "No wind favors him who has no destined port." It takes a certain commitment to be daily in our habits. We intentionally have to stay focused and resist distractions. And when we do, winds will propel us toward the direction of our goals.

We must learn to focus our attention on being consistent *daily*. We need to focus on what matters the most. Distractions are inevitable, but we cannot allow them to dilute our focus and distract us from our destinies. I have discovered that far too often I allow the good to distract me from the best. Only recently did I become disciplined in narrowing my focus.

Darren Hardy, the publisher of *Success* magazine, wrote the book *The Compound Effect*, where he articulates clearly how doing all the little things consistently adds up and helps us reach our goals. Other authors have agreed that you don't have to change *that much* for it to make a great deal of difference. A few simple disciplines can have a major impact on how your life works out in the next ninety days, let alone in the next twelve months or the next three years.

When I was a little boy growing up in Africa, I discovered that I could start a fire using a magnifying glass. All I had to do on a sunny day was to keep the magnifying glass in one position, concentrating the sun's rays in one specific spot. If I waited a few seconds doing only that, I could set a dry leaf on fire. Likewise, when we concentrate our energies on what really matters—one task, one goal, one important aspect of our lives—we can start something powerful. We can get fired up!

> **All I had to do on a sunny day was to keep the magnifying glass in one position, concentrating the sun's rays in one specific spot. If I waited a few seconds doing only that, I could set a dry leaf on fire.**

After reviewing my top-ten list—making loving kindness the top priority, checking thoughts carefully, staying open to lessons, caring for the body, associating with key people, meditating often, being grateful, living on purpose, staying consistent, and honoring commitments—I remind myself that daily disciplines must be written down and that action has to follow awareness.

Goals Must Be Written

Usually at the start of every New Year, various experts are interviewed on TV, radio, or in newspapers, about how to succeed with New Year's resolutions. They all end up giving various suggestions, but one suggestion seems to be a common thread: goals must be written down, and they require a plan of action.

Unless there is discipline, the gap between goals and accomplishment will remain huge. Discipline is a bridge between what we set out to do and what we end up doing in order to get to our destination.

A Harvard study showed that the small percentage of people who write their goals down end up achieving more than all those who don't have written goals. It helps to keep our vision in front of our eyes. Jim Rohn added that the best time to set up a new discipline is when the idea is strong.

I have simplified my goals. I intentionally limit them to seven goals. They are all written down. The first three always have to do with faith, family, and fitness. I print these goals off on a sheet of paper that serves as a bookmark. In addition my checklist is placed in a binder at the very front; that way when I open the binder it is the very first piece of paper that catches my attention.

I print off a number of copies and place them in various journals and my day planner. This way I end up automatically seeing my goals on a daily basis. The vision I have is written and kept in front of me to see. It has been said what we keep before our eyes will affect us. Once our goals are written down, it is easier to see this.

Take Action

Assuming you have pondered your priorities, the things you want to align with the most and the activities that energize you the most; assuming you are aware of your top-ten list; assuming you have actually written it down; and assuming you are aware of how distractions can dilute your focus, then there is one more final step: action.

An affirmation without action is the beginning of delusion. Too many people dream big and write down their visions but lack action. This reminds me of someone who owns a luxury car but lacks the wisdom to put the fuel in that car.

Because I am so busy seeing patients in two clinics, serving on national committees, working as a part-time journalist, training for marathons every day of my life, being a father and a husband and the proud owner of a high-energy dog, I was pleased to discover the value of fifteen minutes. Start small. Take action and be consistent. That is what I learned when I applied the above ideas in brief bursts of fifteen minutes.

Taking action also means that we have to walk the talk, and this begins in the home. I have been taught that nobody likes to be told what to do—especially teenagers. Teens tend to follow our actions more than our words. We owe it to them to at least offer great examples of the benefits of living a disciplined life.

The best time to set up discipline is when the idea is fresh in your mind. If you wait too long, the idea seems less and less appealing. It may actually fade. Or worse someone may steal your idea and run with it before you get to do it yourself.

> **Affirmation without discipline is the beginning of delusion.**

As explained by Winifred Gallagher in *Attention and the Focused Life*, some of us tend to make excuses for our lack of action because we also lack self-discipline:

> Because you actually might not know what activities truly engage your attention and satisfy you, it can be helpful to keep a diary of what you do all day and how you feel while doing it. Then, try to do more of what's rewarding, even if it takes an effort, and less of what isn't. Where optimal experience is concerned, "I just don't have the time," often means "I just don't have the self-discipline."

Become a person of action, and avoid assigning blame. Make no room for excuses, and remember this wisdom of Leonardo da Vinci: "You will never have a greater or lesser dominion than that over yourself ... the height of a man's success is gauged by his self-mastery; the depth of his failure by his self-abandonment ... And this law is the expression of eternal justice. He who cannot establish dominion over himself will have no dominion over others."

Seven Benefits of Discipline

1. Having healthy self-esteem
2. Reaching other goals. All disciplines affect each other. As Helen Keller wrote in *The Story of My Life*, "One painful duty fulfilled makes the next plainer and easier."

3. Fulfilling your destiny
4. Helping others reach their goals and assisting them in moving forward in their lives
5. Living consistently and compassionately
6. Having few regrets. Self-discipline provides a sense of freedom from feeling lazy or lethargic.
7. Creating future breakthroughs, which in turn will inspire you to remain disciplined

Awareness, Taking Action, and Maintaining Discipline

In the end, living a disciplined life boils down to three qualities:

- awareness
- taking action
- maintaining discipline

First become aware of who you are in this world. What is your task here? How do you fit in? Become aware of what some call purpose or destiny. Know what matters the most to you, that which makes you feel aligned with others and that which makes an hour feel like five minutes. In many ways we all suffer from ADD—not an attention deficit but an awareness deficit disorder.

> **We all suffer from some form of ADD—an awareness deficit disorder.**

Then take the hardest step of all: action. So many of us have analysis paralysis where we search for meaning and purpose. We tune it to radio stations that help us grow in all areas of well-being. We try metaphysics, philosophy, faith teachers, books, CDs, courses, online teaching, life coaches, and on and on. Too many of us suffer from metaphysical indigestion, which really means too much information and too little action.

And finally because God allows the teachers to arrive when the students are ready, we arrive at a place where daily discipline becomes a habit. Maintaining this behavior not only benefits us but also those who are open to grow with us as we live our purpose and serve others.

Discipline comes effortless when we are inspired by our Creator and when we are in sync with our destinies. But like a suntan, it requires consistent exposure to the right ideas and people. As soon as we move away from our source, our excuses increase while our discipline fades like a tan fades in chronically cloud-covered locations far away from the sunny equator.

Simple indeed … but not easy to do unless we truly have the desire to move forward, be inspired, inspire others, serve them, and live out our purpose.

We can move forward after facing setbacks, and we can maintain a healthy balance of our mental, physical, and spiritual energies. But how do we do all of that consistently? In the next chapter I shall take a closer look at the benefits of consistency.

Action Steps

1. *Make the time intentionally to list your billiard balls, your pebbles, and your sand.* Only you have the right amount of information to do that. Nobody else can do it for you. Figure out what works best for you. A good time to "huddle" over these thoughts could be Sunday nights—at the end of the weekend and before the next week kicks off. Narrow your focus. The important things are often threatened by the urgent. Having too many irons in the fire potentially can dilute your discipline and distract you from your dharma or destiny.

2. *Reflect on what you want the most.* What do you want more? Is it fitness or nice but unhealthy foods? Is it the book you always wanted to write or the relaxing TV programs at night that you "deserve" after a long day at work?

3. *Use checklists.* Remember that the *d* in discipline means *daily.* Using simple checklists is one of the best ways to stay consistent.

Being disciplined also means that you must give your attention to the details that lubricate your heart. So have a daily desire to pay attention to the right details.

4. *Stay accountable.* Although some people have a tremendous amount of self-discipline, they are the exception. Most of us do better when we have someone whom we trust to keep us accountable. I've heard it said, "Everyone needs a coach, even the best among us." (I cannot thank David Irvine enough for keeping me accountable when I told him about this book.)

5. *Consider your mind and mouth.* Since everything begins with a single thought, it is important to guard your thoughts. That takes daily discipline. Remind yourself frequently that CAN'T stands for *can't allow negative thinking.*

6. *Be certain of your destiny.* The more you know your purpose, the more likely it is that you will stay focused, disciplined, and on track. If you are clear on the why, the how will show up. Distractions will come, but you will be able to refocus sharply because you want to fulfill your purpose. Disciplined living is not about a destination; it is about the journey. How you see yourself determines how you experience this incredible journey.

7. *Look back at times in the past when you succeeded at being disciplined.* Why did you succeed? What did you do? Were there patterns you can learn from? Learn from your previous successes, and know that if you were disciplined once, you can be disciplined again. I tend to match areas I want to be more disciplined in with areas where I've already succeeded. For example, I have been running every day since 2009, and that takes discipline. I try to match my writing with my running, and so far it is working well.

Chapter 4

Consistency

In consistency lies the power.
—Author unknown

Moving forward is one of the most important decisions we can make in life, because it allows us to grow, learn new lessons, have more energy, enjoy more peace, and overcome our adversities. It takes courage to overcome adversity and to grow from our experiences, and it takes discipline to establish healthy routines. We have to stretch beyond our comfort zone and let go of the past. My work as a physician has taught me that people get sick when they cannot let go of past pains; they struggle to move on. Fear of the unknown derails many from their lives' purposes—instead of moving forward, some decide to stay in the same situation.

I am told a locomotive can be held back by one brick if it is stationary. Once it has momentum, a brick wall cannot hold it back. How do we establish momentum? What are some ways to become relentlessly consistent? How do we overcome procrastination? In this chapter I will present ways consistent living helps us move forward.

The hardest part of exercise is putting on running shoes and tying up our laces. Being on a quest to run at least one hundred marathons, I can attest to that—especially when it snows outside, when it is dark, and when strong winds slam frigid flakes right into my eyes. Many athletes are motivated by the slogan Just Do It, used by Nike, a company named after the Greek goddess of victory. When we change our intentions from inertia to doing something, we move closer to our victories. Without consistency the odds of victory melt away like an ice cube under the noon sun.

Once the decision has been made to move forward, the battle is half-won. Turning back is harder, similar to when we have tied our shoelaces and are heading out the door. It's a matter of taking action *now*. It is all about staying in the present, refusing to turn back, and refusing to quit; our goal is to move forward each and every day.

After close to three decades of working in a medical clinic and seeing thousands of patients who want to change their lifestyles and live healthier and longer, I am convinced that the difference between success and failure comes down to one single word: *consistency*. Many start this journey with good intentions, but somewhere along the path they get distracted or complacent. Some quit and end their quest to reach their ideal weight.

My question to you is, What do you value so intensely that you are prepared to do something about it on a daily basis? Do you *really* understand fully what "You cannot change what you are prepared to tolerate" means? In my own journey I've always valued healthy habits, but I was not always consistent.

In 2009 I decided to run every day for the rest of my life. This decision has taught me much about the benefits of consistency. When I observe people who live with consistency in mind, I have noticed that many share these common qualities:

- keeping goals simple yet specific
- always recalibrating when facing distractions or obstacles
- staying focused on motives and priorities
- encouraging themselves with positive affirmations
- avoiding procrastination by starting small
- having deadlines and being accountable
- above all enjoying the journey—having fun

The Meeting—Simplify

A number of experts met at an obesity conference one day. Being tired and bored after seeing thousands of colorful, complicated PowerPoint slides, they decided to take a break. Enjoying some food and beverages, they brainstormed and asked some important what-if questions. What if they forgot about all the complicated science explaining the causes and treatments of obesity and focused on patients who were successful? What if all the successful patients were enrolled in a registry? What if success was defined as losing 10 percent of one's body weight and keeping that off for at least one year? What if these patients were then tracked over a number of subsequent years to see what made some successful over a *lifetime*?

The National Weight Control Registry was conceived, and the results were simple yet very revealing. Consistency was one of the main reasons for success in reaching and maintaining the ideal weight.

Those weight controllers who were able to start their journey *and* finish strong did only six things, but they did them consistently:

- They got active and stayed active, taking at least ten thousand steps (five miles or eight kilometers) per day.
- They never skipped breakfast.
- They decided on a realistic meal plan and stuck with that plan day after day, regardless of where they lived or traveled. The various meal plans ranged from low fats to low carbohydrates to a predominantly plant-based diet. They were able to reduce both their fat intake and overall caloric intake.
- They weighed themselves once a week in order to closely monitor any changes—both up or down.
- They were quick to correct mistakes or carelessness—especially during the holiday seasons (Christmas and Thanksgiving are notorious disruptions of well-laid plans.)

For more information about the registry, visit www.nwcr.ws.

The Flight Path—Recalibrate

A few years ago I had lunch with my friend Jim Hunter. Jim is a former Canadian Olympic athlete in downhill skiing and sometimes goes by the name of Jungle Jim. Our lunch took place on a dreary, gray day. A strong wind flung flurries against the window close to our table—a typical prairie storm racing fiercely into our city and causing havoc in traffic. One word on the front page of the paper that day said it all: "Walloped!"

Later that day I was supposed to fly south to do a talk at a medical conference. I was looking forward to escaping from the frigid fury of Mother Nature. A much warmer environment was awaiting me. Jim knew about my travel plans and asked me a very profound question: "Peter, when you are cruising later today in that jet what percentage of the time will the pilot follow the flight path?" I pondered, looking at the strong winds outside and calculating my answer …

"At least ninety-nine percent of the time," I answered, thinking of all my previous flights all over the planet. Then I added, "All the previous pilots got me to my destination!"

"It's only three percent," Jim responded. I was curious as to how that could be and asked Jim to explain.

His explanation made total sense to me, and once you see it too, my hope is that it may give you courage to do what must be done in whatever area it is you want to be more consistent.

> In life it is inevitable that distractions will dilute your focus, that fatigue will make you careless, and that obstacles will loom large.

Here is the answer: using their skills and with the help of critical instruments, pilots are quick to correct the planes' courses once winds or other weather conditions impact the flight paths.

The point here is that in life it is inevitable that distractions will dilute our focus, that fatigue will make us careless, and that unforeseen obstacles will loom large. Our best supporters may tell us it is time to give up, and our doubts and fears will shout louder than our faith. But it is during those times that we have to bring our metaphorical planes back to the ideal flight path—the longer we wait, the harder it is to remain on task and finish strong. We may well move forward but end up at the wrong destination.

Focus

A few years ago I tuned in to the breakfast television show that I contributed to regularly, trying to get a flavor of the current focus of the show's producers. I always tried to match my medical segments to the "DNA" of morning television—aiming to remain not only entertaining but also relevant.

A gymnast and gold medal winner at the Athens Olympic Games was the guest, and he was asked, "What is the biggest predictor of success?" Without thinking too long, he confidently stated, "Focus." When asked, "What is the biggest predictor of failure?" he responded even quicker by saying, "Doubt." To truly focus, consistency is vital if we are to move forward. Distractions are inevitable, but focus is not optional. To succeed, one needs relentless focus similar to the singular focus of a magnifying glass which can start a fire.

> **When asked, "What is the biggest predictor of failure?" he answered, "Doubt."**

In life, our consistent focus on the most important priorities will enable us to move forward.

Not only does singular focus help us to be consistent, but consistent actions also depend on the affirmations we use. Our most influential muscle is in our mouth.

One Powerful Muscle—Positive Affirmations

I once heard a wise teacher say, "Feed your faith and doubt your doubts." It is easier said than done. One way to do this is to watch what comes out of our mouths. Our affirmations reflect our thoughts and beliefs. The most powerful muscle may be in our thighs, but the most influential muscle may be our tongue. Our words and affirmations carry energy—more than most of may realize before we start paying attention to our words.

I learned from the wise teacher the same truth I learned from the Olympic athlete: we must have focus, and we must avoid doubt. You cannot believe for success and continuously affirm failure. Be consistent in your focus in terms of what you believe, expect, say, and think.

Think of a target. When aiming at it we may miss it, hit it on the edge, or hit it dead center for a bull's eye. *That* must be our focus—to hit goals dead center as we strive to move forward consistently.

Will we always strike the target dead center? Obviously not. But as Wayne Gretzky said, you have to shoot the puck at the net if you want to score. It may not go in always, but at least shoot consistently. Aim consistently, and don't have the disconnect of believing one thing and then speaking the opposite. Our affirmations have power—more than we may realize. Use that power to work for you, not against you.

Start Where You Are

A recent report in *Harvard Business Review* outlined consistent qualities that researchers at Harvard observed in so-called *high-potential employees*. These individuals were in the top 3–5 percent of all the staff working for various companies. These high-potential employees all started somewhere at the bottom of the ladder.

The report revealed some of the following observations:

- These employees delivered results consistently and solved problems superbly.
- They had a nose for opportunity and took risks, but at the same time they skirted away from unwise risks.

- They were all relentless learners.
- As they moved up the ladder, they developed new expertise.
- At first they were great at fitting in with others, but subsequently they became wonderful role models and teachers.
- They had the drive to excel and achieve more. They were hungry for growth and improvement.

Another common thread was that all the above virtues were executed consistently.

Although it's always inspiring to read about these kinds of achievers, it is even more fun to meet one of them in person. I met such a person in the boardroom of his car dealership a while ago. Gerry Woods, originally from Scotland, came to Canada in the late seventies and started to sell cars. Gerry was originally a salesman at a well-known dealership, and after five years he decided to step into new shoes—acquiring his own dealership. I asked him why he made that choice while some of his peers settled for the comfortable place, still selling cars as opposed to being the owner of multiple car dealerships.

At first Gerry joked by saying, "I was dumb enough and did not know how much risk was involved." But then he paused and wryly observed, "They did not have any drive or desire. They lacked focus." Today, Gerry is respected in a city of over one million people and has four hundred employees. He is charitable to those in need and mentors key employees to take over from him later when the time is right.

What I admire about successful people in the business world is that their methods of operation can teach us as parents, athletes, and coaches how to bring out the best in others and ourselves: many successful individuals simply started where they were, but they consistently made the choices to move forward and live their lives by intent and not by accident.

The Early Years Set the Wellness Stage

One of the joys of being a pediatrician is to help others see the value of starting early in our quest to remain consistent. I have observed that the healthiest patients consistently cultivate healthy habits. When it comes to living to one hundred, most experts will tell us that our genes make the biggest difference. Although that may be true, I have also observed after many years of clinical work that lifestyle matters at least as much. Some days I think lifestyle matters even more. The science of epigenetics seems to confirm this.

When I saw newborns in the hospital where I took call for over twenty-five years, I always made the point when I left the room to tell the new parents, "Your child will live to one hundred." I was quick to add a caveat: "*If*, from a young age, he or she consistently eats right, exercises consistently, watches his or her weight carefully, controls stress, avoids toxins such as cigarette smoke, and keeps his or her heart filled with gratitude and forgiveness."

> **When it comes to longevity, lifestyle matters as much as our genes—if not more.**

I read about a journalist from Montreal, writing for the *Le Devoir* newspaper, who went to Okinawa, an island south of Japan with 1.3 million inhabitants. Her goal was to see why so many inhabitants live to well over one hundred years. Logically it made sense to look at the children first, and here is what she discovered:

- They ate healthy fruits, vegetables, fish, and significantly less sugary foods compared to children in North America. They also ate less fats and certainly not even french fries once in a while.
- They contributed toward keeping their classrooms clean. They washed the floors and cleaned toilets. There were no caretakers. They were taught the value of responsibility at a young age.
- The teachers made a point of letting the children play outside for at least twenty minutes.

While the children were playing, the journalist asked the teacher if there were any children with hyperactivity (attention deficit disorders). The teacher was surprised by the question. The reporter had to explain her question once more by asking if medication was ever used to affect the brains of children so they could learn better. The teacher was horrified and answered, "Of course not. Why would we do that to our children?" The teachers understood the value of healthy lifestyle choices taught to children at a young age.

Similar to the children in Okinawa, physical activity taught at an early age and enforced consistently in the later years can set the stage. A few years ago in Ontario I was honored to hear Olympian Silken Laumann give the keynote speech at the annual meeting of the Canadian Pediatric Society.

Silken achieved major breakthroughs as a rower for Canada in the 1992 Olympic Games by winning a bronze medal—this after she had to overcome what looked like a career-ending injury. She followed up her passion for rowing with passion for getting kids more active. She started the charity Active Kids Movement in 2003 and also wrote a book, *Child's Play: Rediscovering the Joy of Play in Our Families and Communities*. This Olympian is helping children all over the world to get active and stay active. By starting at a young age the goal is to set the stage for consistent lifestyle habits in the years ahead.

I cannot think of anything more basic and worthwhile as starting children on a consistent exercise plan and a healthy eating schedule. I am stunned that exercise and eating healthy are rarely seen as investments that parents can make into their children's futures.

Sometimes I meet people who did not have parents who taught them to start early with the quest of becoming more consistent in watering the seeds of healthy living. They ask me if it's ever too late. I tell them not at all. It's never too late to become more aware of the power of consistent, healthy choices.

The Sunday Huddle Routine

In the former pediatric weight clinic that I cofounded in Calgary, I taught families the importance of a Sunday-night huddle. Football players always huddle as a team prior to executing key plays. I encouraged families to set aside a few minutes each Sunday night to huddle—to go over their four to five goals for the week ahead. The world-renowned motivational teacher Zig Ziglar teaches that one should focus on only four or five goals at a time. The Chinese even narrow it down to *one*. They have a proverb that says, "He who chases after two rabbits will catch none."

It helps to write goals down and leave them on the fridge where you can constantly see them. Visual reminders serve many of us the best. Out of sight often means out of mind.

I encourage you to set aside thirty minutes to plan ahead for the coming week. In addition to written goals you may also want to use a green elastic band around your wrist as a reminder to stay consistent in executing your goals. Green is a symbolic color for new beginnings. I have designed a green wristband that says, "Believe, Expect, Speak and Think Positive." I call it my BEST-living reminder. I made it mostly as a reminder for myself to live by those few words every day of the week as long as possible after my own Sunday huddles. Its physical presence serves as a visible reminder, thus making me more consistent in planning how I want to move forward each day.

When I see families in the weight-management clinic, I encourage them to keep things simple yet consistent.

Here is what I share:

- Have a customized plan for the family, and write it down. The best time to do this may be on Sunday nights. Keep this huddle time realistic. It should not take more than fifteen to thirty minutes each week

- Your plan must be in a checklist format. The value of checklists, whatever the area of living may be, was well illustrated by the *New York Times* best seller *The Checklist Manifesto*, by young, dynamic Harvard surgeon Dr. Atul Gawande.

- The main reasons for inconsistencies in our lives are simple: distractions and complacency. In order to deal with these inevitable events I suggest to patients to think about parking spots. Parking spots close to the shopping mall on a busy day are often taken, and the parking spot assigned to the CEO at work is reserved so nobody else can park there. We have to consistently prioritize our top goals. My point is simply this: once a spot is taken, it is taken. So have your sacred time slot—like a reserved parking spot—consistently marked out. For some it may be just after supper each night.

The main reason for inconsistencies in our lives is simple: distractions. In order to deal with these inevitable events, have your huddle time clearly marked out, like a reserved parking spot.

Establish Daily Rhythms

Just like bookends holding up books, I have found over the years that when I pay attention to what I read just before I switch the lights off at night and soon after I wake up, I am "held" together. How we start and end our days matter a great deal

For example, on my bedside table I keep some key books that I scan—even for as briefly as one minute—when I am tired at night

---

Just like bookends holding up books, I have found over the years that when I pay attention to what I read just before I switch the lights off at night and soon after I wake up, I am "held" together.

For some of us it may not be a book. It may be a quote. Perhaps it is a poem. For others it is a note of encouragement someone sent them. Make it a habit to not allow any negative ideas—especially the evening news—to enter your mind before you drift off to sleep. When you do that, you will sleep better and end up with more energy and also more ideas. The more ideas you get, the more you will be able to consistently move forward, endure adversity, and live out your calling and passions.

Darren Hardy, publisher of *Success* magazine says he uses his iPhone alarm to wake him up. He deliberately uses the snooze bar to get a few extra minutes—not to sleep but to intentionally go through a list of things to be grateful for. It is a great idea. Recently, while on a road trip, I tried it with my iPhone. It works. Gratefulness at the start makes the rest of the day go much better.

I like to grow daily in wisdom and understanding. Thus I consistently cultivate the habit of reading for a few minutes as soon as I wake up. First I read the Bible, which I consider a book of wisdom. Then I study words written by one of my spiritual mentors. I have made a point to pause and meditate immediately following this ritual.

Only after that do I scan the newspaper to see what happened while I slept peacefully. This consistent habit equips me to know what both the spiritual and physical worlds are up to. This is something Zig Ziglar taught me. Zig also said, "If you keep on doing what you have been doing, you will keep on getting what you have been getting."

Use morning meditation tools to start your days off right, and end the days with positive affirmations. Do that consistently and your life will shine. You will bring light to others by becoming enlightened yourself first. We cannot give what we do not have, but by establishing consistent daily patterns, we accumulate skills that can serve others better.

Be Sure of Your Motives—Have a Huge Why

I love learning from men and women who had their backs against the wall at one point of their lives and then turned things around to the point where they become our heroes and role models. These individuals taught me that consistency played a key role in them becoming successful.

A few years ago, I met a successful multimillionaire, Bob Burdick, in Phoenix where my wife and I attended a conference on nutrition. Bob worked as a drywaller and battled hard to feed his big family.

I remember seeing some photos of Bob struggling to make ends meet. He lived in a tiny trailer with very little space. There was no running water, let alone a washroom for him, his wife, and five children.

That poverty came to an end when Bob was introduced to a business plan where he could determine his own income. He soon arrived at a point where the idea of residual income became the driver for his hard work. He accepted the invitation of another businessman who taught him how to live the dream of making money by helping people live healthier lives. Bob's passion to serve and support other businessmen remains his motive to this day. Consistent planning fuels his passions.

Today Bob is a multimillionaire who makes money in his sleep, because he had a solid reason for getting out of poverty—he loved his family dearly. That was one of his whys. But there was another why. He asked himself, "How may I serve others?"

Bob was not motivated by selfishness. He bought into the notion taught by many lifestyle coaches that in life you can get anything you want if you just help enough people get what they want. Today when one hears Bob talk about his goals—he still has many goals despite his many past successes—it is clear that he is where he is because he has a passion that motivates him to be consistent in talking to others about what he can do to help them live healthier. I was not surprised to hear him count the days until the next meeting where he would continue to help many others move forward too by becoming financially independent.

Have Fun

I am blessed with a curious mind, and I enjoy asking questions and learning from others all the time. I have always admired Larry King for his ability to ask good questions. His curiosity is inspiring. I always picture him as sitting behind a microphone with his trademark suspenders, leaning forward in anticipation of what the guests will say next. The show is now off the air, but there is no doubt it was one of the most influential shows in CNN's repertoire at one stage. The show was simple, consistent, and entertaining.

Watching the show, I noticed a pattern. Many of the guests were having fun doing what they felt called to do. They lived lives that illustrate what *Moving Forward* is all about. They were people who overcame adversity. They associated with wise teachers. They looked after their health in order to have the energy to still do what they enjoyed doing. They had consistent goals and were careful in watering the right seeds. They learned from their failures, and they maintained a daily discipline. Above all they were motivated by loving kindness and compassion.

When they were independently asked the same question, a question that Larry King loved to ask, "Will you ever retire?" the vast majority said, "Not really … I am having too much fun. You know what it's like, Larry. I don't do this for the money anymore … I do it because it is fun." It is indeed easier to sustain a career that energizes you. I feel blessed to be able to help families live healthy lives, and I enjoy every day in my clinic.

> **When asked "Will you ever retire?" the vast majority said, "Not really … I am having too much fun. I don't do this for money anymore … I do it because it is fun."**

Being a pediatrician I am always amused by kids being very authentic and honest. That is why Art Linkletter, the host of the former widely popular TV show *Kids Say the Darndest Things,* caught my attention when he was a guest on Larry King. Linkletter was born in Moose Jaw, Saskatchewan. His biological mom abandoned him and left him by the stairs outside a church. Linkletter was adopted by a minister who later moved from Moose Jaw to California.

Linkletter passed away in 2010, almost making it to one hundred years of age. After reading his obituary I was struck by how much he enjoyed his work as an entertainer and journalist. Not only did he make others laugh, but he also could laugh at himself for the mistakes he made.

One such mistake was when his friend Walter told him to buy a piece of land next to an amusement park Walter was planning to build. Although Linkletter and his friend Walter knew each other well and liked each other, there was only one problem: Walter had failed too often with all his previous business deals. So Linkletter respectfully declined.

That was a huge mistake, because we know Walter as Walt Disney. Had Linkletter followed his friend's advice, he would have made millions more! I remember the mischievous grin on his face when he told Larry King about his "silly mistake." In addition to being a great entertainer, respected by many, Linkletter was also known for all the successful investments he consistently made over a lifetime. He knew how to have fun doing what he did, and he did that consistently for decades

Having fun means that we are certain of our passions. We may start small, but we grow over the years, and we value consistency. Prosperity is not a level of income; it is a consciousness. Those of us who became deeply conscious of the power of consistency also became prosperous. We share this prosperity as we move forward by serving others, all the while following our own calling.

Recently I had the honor to visit with a prosperous person while returning from a medical conference in Toronto. John Stanton, founder of the Running Room stores in North America, travels 260 days a year for work. I was in the airport lounge at Toronto's Pearson Airport when I heard John's booming voice declare, "They should not allow guys like you in this lounge." Not only does he have a great sense of humor, but John also knows how to lead his company to consistent growth.

He always inspires me with his wisdom and energy. John's approach to staying motivated is to keep his exercise routine gentle enough that he does not get injured and progressive enough that he shows improvement. Most importantly John keeps his workouts fun. He believes that if you are not having fun, you are not doing it right. I could not agree more, and I can honestly say that my habit of running every day of my life is fueled by me having fun whenever I get to enjoy the privilege of physical activity.

I run daily not only because it's fun but also because I have decided that it's a priority and enough of a priority to do it early in the day, before I have less and less control over my schedule. Some days there are unexpected calls from journalists for interviews; other days medical emergencies force me to put patients before my own needs. Then there are days that are just so demanding that by the time I get home, I am too tired to lace up my running shoes—even more tired than waking up in the morning after getting insufficient sleep. The fun of creating daily energy keeps me consistent.

Know Your Top-Ten List

I have been honored to see how the American Academy of Pediatrics functions. I was asked to serve as their representative leader from Alberta, Canada. This allowed me to attend the academy's annual leadership forum (ALF) in Chicago.

Meetings take place over several days, and at the end of it all the academy comes up with ten key resolutions. Examples may be to take action regarding children's oral health or early mental development, or perhaps the Academy wants to reduce the incidence of overweight children. The key point, however, is that after hours and hours of hard work, the board decides on a top-ten list.

I have also worked with other national organizations that did not have top-ten lists. They claimed their successes were rather minor because of the smaller size of their organizations. They had it all wrong. They functioned below potential because they lacked top-ten lists. Their understanding of the value of consistency was rudimentary at best.

Here is a question to consider: What is your organization or family's top-ten list? If you don't have one yet, it's never too late to start, and once you do start, be sure to keep the momentum alive with consistency.

Have Deadlines

I've heard it said, "A goal without a deadline is a dream." That may well be true. Certainly as I get closer to my goal of running one hundred marathons by age sixty, I can truly say that without deadlines I would not be as far ahead.

I have had the honor to write for two newspapers—one local and one national. The editors have given me consistent deadlines. It works well. I always completed my articles on time. I was far, far less consistent in my book-writing endeavors, until I was kept accountable by another author, Dave Irvine. My book was always a dream until I set a deadline.

Unless you have a deadline where you can review your progress, you will fail; you will only dream, and success will elude you. Why not consider doing what Ben Franklin did? Every week for thirteen weeks he worked on one task. He did that in four cycles each year. It is simple but not easy, because it does not come naturally for most of us. But once we establish a consistent system, as Franklin did, we can move forward with purpose.

It is important to have a system in which we make appointments with ourselves. Make an appointment once a week. Set an alarm. With the help of new smartphones and numerous apps we can tap into new technology.

Every week these tools can remind us that it is time for the review. Once again remember the Sunday huddle.

Even though deadlines keep us consistent, some goals should not have deadlines. They are lifelong. Take, for example, the goal of always ensuring that in a world where we cannot control everything we at least have *full* control of our attitudes. The saying "Our attitude is everything" is indeed very true, and paying attention to it consistently determines our destiny and direction. Yet when we know the things we know, some of us consistently fail to do the things we know we ought to do. We seem to get distracted by the inevitable ups and downs of our lives. Even when we *know* that our attitude determines our energy level, our ability to persist, and the quality of our relationships, we *allow* what we know to get derailed by distractions.

On a recent flight I was honored to have a businessman with an amazingly positive attitude as a seatmate. I really enjoy flying for many reasons, but the top reason for the joy is that my best ideas often come from fellow travelers. I recognized my seatmate as one of my unexpected but divinely appointed teachers. He explained the nature and potential of his business to me with great excitement. But one thing he said stood out: "Inches leads to yardage." He was saying that small, incremental changes in the right direction add up. One can apply this wisdom to any area of life. My impression that consistency provides clarity was confirmed at thirty-five thousand feet.

Consistency keeps us on the proper flight path. In the next chapter I will look at why the people and organizations we align with matter so much in our quest to move forward.

Action Steps

1. *This coming Sunday start a habit of setting aside thirty minutes to huddle.* Make an appointment with yourself—enter it in your day planner, or write it on a list you keep of things to do. Consider using the alarm on your smartphone to remind you of this critical decision.

2. *Intentionally set time aside to reflect on* only three *areas of your life where you desire to become more consistent.* The more areas you work on at once, the less likely you will be successful. Keep things simple and specific.

3. *Get a journal and a pen or use your favorite electronic device to record the three areas you have chosen.* Perhaps, if you are like most others, your goals will be related to health, relationships, or finances. All three are common areas where we want to finish strong.

4. *Once recorded, make sure to keep your goals in a place where you will see them repeatedly.* Consider regular reviews in the morning and before bedtime. Reviews must be done daily; otherwise your goals will remain only a wish list written down, tucked away somewhere, literally in the dark, and ultimately unfruitful.

5. *Use the Ben Franklin method of working on a task over thirteen weeks.* That way, by being consistently focused, you can go over four cycles each year.

6. *If you make a mistake—and most of us will—remember pilots follow the exact flight path only 3 percent of the time.* Be realistic and take a long-term view; be quick to correct your mistakes.

7. *Use visual reminders such as colored wristbands.* You may need to change to another colored wristband in order to set new goals.

8. *Remember that your attitude toward your mind, body, and spirit determines what you become.* Facing this truth takes courage. Doing something about what you want to improve may be birthed in pain if your attitude is "This is what I *have* to do." But when you instead affirm, "This is what I *get* to do," it gets birthed in the pleasure of finding your true purpose and calling.

CHAPTER 5

ASSOCIATIONS

A man only learns in two ways, one by reading and
the other by associating with smarter people.
—Will Rogers

A well-known saying states that we will be known by the company we keep. The Bible puts it plainly: to become wise, spend time with the wise. It has been a privilege for me to associate with wise people who bring out the absolute best in me. When I reflect on how my associations have enabled me to move forward, I am honored to go back in memory to a recent visit to Washington DC.

This city is one of my favorite places to visit. Some of my most memorable runs have been by the National Mall, passing iconic landmarks such as the Lincoln Memorial, where I once stopped and read the words uttered by Abraham Lincoln, one of the most respected presidents in American history. These words continue to impress me:

> With malice toward none, with charity for all, with firmness in the right as God gives us to see the right, let us strive on to finish the work we are in, to bind up the nation's wounds, to care for him who shall have borne the battle and for his widow and his orphan, to do all which may achieve and cherish a just and lasting peace among ourselves and with all nations.

One recent morning, I ran by the reflecting pool by the Lincoln Memorial, but this time I was not alone. My friend Dr. Dan Kirschenbaum, a well-respected and influential psychologist, was in town for an international obesity conference. Dan has always brought out the best in me. Many of my medical skills caring for overweight patients come from Dan, who has been generous in sharing his wisdom. As Isaac Newton famously observed, "If I have seen further, it is by standing on the shoulders of giants." Dan is one of those giants who has graciously allowed me to stand on his shoulders.

While we were running, I told him I felt like the mule that entered the Kentucky Derby: although victory was very improbable, the association did the mule some good. He was kind enough to reassure me that I was not a mule and that I did indeed bring some useful thoughts to the table.

Charles Schultz once said, "Life is like a ten-speed bicycle. We all have gears we do not use." Dan makes those who associate with him use all their gears. He always seems to bring out the best in others.

I also visit my friend Gerrie Botha when I am in Washington, DC. I have known him since childhood, and we have stayed in touch for over five decades. He was a lawyer with the World Bank, and the fact that the bank sent him to numerous venues all over the world speaks volumes— they trust him. A quote, attributed to William Arthur Ward, summarizes our friendship: "A true friend knows your weaknesses, but shows you your strengths; feels your fears, but fortifies your faith; sees your anxieties, but frees your spirit; recognizes your disabilities, but emphasizes your possibilities."

I'll never forget what Gerrie taught me when we were playing tennis as high school kids one day under the sunny skies of Africa. He wisely observed, as a fifteen-year-old, "Life is God's gift to us, and what we do with our lives is our gift back to God." Since we learn from our friends, our associations with others become that much more meaningful. Not only do we grow, but we also encourage others to move forward too.

> **Life is God's gift to us, and what we do with our lives is our gift back to God.**
> **—Gerrie Botha**

On a lighter note, Gerrie's sense of humor always seems to bless me at times when I need to lighten up. I recently went through a season where I needed to laugh a bit more and frown less. Just at the right time—when I *really* needed to be cheered up—a great joke arrived in my inbox from Gerrie. It was a joke about two medical school friends who wanted to set up a clinic where they shared some space. One doctor was a proctologist and the other a psychiatrist. They struggled to find the right way to promote themselves and finally settled on the idea of looking after odds and ends.

As shown by the two illustrations of how my friends have impacted me, who we associate with matters much. Positive associations bring out the best in us. We preserve our energy when we avoid *basement* people— those who pull us down. We function with higher energy when we instead associate with *balcony* people who thrive when lifting others up. It is important to choose these associations wisely if we are to successfully reach our goals. Our associations shape our attitudes. Healthy associations enable us to move forward; we triumph over troubles together and obliterate obstacles as a team.

Mark Twain said, "Keep away from people who belittle your ambitions. Small people always do that, but the really great make you feel that you too can become great." We must avoid these small people at all costs. They are not on our team. Some may sit in the front seat when we are on stage, but their body language radiates nothing but negative energy toward us. I call them *turkeys* because they are good at bugging us, but only if we allow them. If you are a true *eagle*, turkeys cannot soar high with you.

It has been said that our associations with human beings steer us into self-observation. It is by observing more of ourselves that we grow. Proverbs, a book of wisdom in the Bible, talks about how we are like iron sharpening iron when we learn from others and help each other grow. In this chapter I will look deeper into how our associations help us in our journeys forward.

Leaders

Associating with leaders can be one of the best investments you ever make. Author and speaker John Maxwell has written extensively about leadership. He has sold more than twenty million books, and his organization has trained more than five million leaders in 153 countries. Some of his books made it to the *New York Times* Best Seller list and stayed there for weeks.

John also does monthly interviews with *Success* magazine. I heard him tell Darren Hardy, the publisher and founding editor of *Success,* that if one were to boil down the definition of leadership to one word, that word would be *influence.* This simple but powerful word defines leadership well.

While cleaning out my study recently I came across a list describing the differences between a boss and a leader. This piece of wisdom was filed in the bottom of a drawer, but it should really have been at the top. I now keep it in a more strategic and visible spot to remind me of its truths.

The Difference

A Boss …	A Leader …
drives his employees	coaches them
assigns slavery	sets the pace
inspires fear	inspires enthusiasm
says, "Get here on time"	beats them to getting there
depends on authority	depends on goodwill
makes work drudgery	makes it interesting
assigns blame for breakdowns	fixes the breakdowns
may not know how to do it	always knows and shows how
uses *I*	uses *we*
says, "Go!"	says, "Let's go!"

I often enjoy reading in the business section of the *Wall Street Journal* or the *New York Times* where people talk about how proud they are of the companies they work at. Often it has to do with working for a great leader who leads by coaching, by example, and by inspiring the team with his or her enthusiasm.

I heard someone say that because she does not have a formal leadership role these ideas may not apply to her. Let me tell you about the mother who saw me recently with her picky eater. She was clearly frustrated after meeting with a registered dietician at our local children's hospital, which is also academically affiliated with the medical school.

She told me how this dietitian had treated her as if she knew nothing. She said, "Dr. Nieman, you should have been there to see how condescending this lady was. I almost felt like leaving the room." Clearly this clinician made a common mistake in her role as a leader. She failed to first ask some basic questions and then meet the mother where she was at. She did not start with what the mother already knew. Had the dietitian done that, just maybe she could have led this mother to a place of excitement about ways to improve the family's eating habits. Getting alongside others, meeting them where they are at, and leading them forward is not a new concept. Many years ago in China a wise sage, Lao-Tzu, came up with this idea: "Go to the people. Live among the people. Learn from them. Start with what they know. Build on what they have. But of the best leaders when their task is accomplished, the people will say 'We have done it ourselves.'"

The point is we all are leaders, and when we associate with good leaders, we become better. We move forward, we grow, and we end up helping others reach their goals.

Influencers

While at a medical meeting in Florida a few years ago I witnessed a most boring lecture, given by one of the smartest clinicians in the area of obesity. His slides were useless, not practical, and complicated to follow, and the delivery style was as exciting as watching paint dry. (My goal here is not to judge critically but to point out my compassion for this expert who was smart yet had a diminished influence due to his inability to keep his audience engaged.)

My mind started to wander. I remembered another speaker at a nutrition conference in Memphis. This man was witty. He talked about how he'd struggled to give good speeches when he was inexperienced. He explained, "My first talk was so bad that if I was not the speaker, I would have walked out!"

As I continued listening to the obesity expert, my mind kept on wandering. I was bored. Within five minutes I came up with a list of twenty qualities I have noticed in people who are influential. These are people who use all their gifts and talents in ways that create win-win situations: they are smart, but they also know how to communicate.

The following are the twenty qualities I see in influential people:

1. Influencers are clever and smart. They get things fast. They can also recall relevant data and stories in no time. It is their nature.

2. They know how to express themselves. They are articulate and use stories to move and inspire people. How delightful it was recently for me to hear a speaker talk about social marketing (the science of helping others make healthy decisions) in the context of getting others to wear helmets when they cycle, to stop smoking, to exercise, and to get immunized. She was a great communicator, and the reason why was simple: she used humor and stories appropriately. Her audience was mesmerized by her influential ideas.

3. Influencers have a high EQ (emotional quotient.) In other words, they can read people wisely, are charismatic, and know how to work a room.

4. They care about their outer appearance by dressing appropriately. Their clothes may not be bought in Milan, but they fit well and are clean and appropriately color coordinated.

5. They have a sense of humor. Their humor is discreet so that it does not offend. As a result it does not reduce the respect the audience has for them. They never share off-color jokes.

6. They believe passionately in what they are talking about. One can tell they are 100 percent involved in what they have to say. Their motives are to serve. Dr. Mehmet Oz, winner of a number of Emmy Awards for his dynamic TV show, illustrates this kind of passion.

7. Influencers are disciplined and rarely distracted by that which is irrelevant. They have a singular, laser-sharp focus on what really matters.

8. They avoid giving those they want to influence too much information. It is hard to drink from a fire hydrant. Influencers understand that well.

9. They are able to identify whom to connect with. They always are working on improving their networking skills.

10. Influencers are original and therefore stand out. They bring something new and relevant to the table. They always remain authentic.

11. They are healthy and beam out vitality. Dr. Oz always looks rested and joyful when he enters the studio, dressed in a comfortable sports jacket and wearing no tie.

12. They are friendly and smile frequently. They pay attention to their body language. It is easy for them to be authentic—as opposed to faking it. Joel Osteen has been accused of smiling too much. He is known as "the smiling pastor." It does not bother him in the least ... he just keeps on smiling!

13. Influencers are highly organized. They rarely waste any time. This gives them great confidence. Stephen Covey, author of *The 7 Habits of Highly Effective People*, never wasted time. His obituary in the *New York Times* included a story of Covey brushing his teeth, shaving, and having a shower all at the same time!

14. Their resources always meet the needs of their audience. One of America's most influential pediatricians is Dr. William Sears. His numerous books illustrate this point clearly. When I showed my mother in Cape Town Dr. Sears's book *Primetime Health*, she could not put it down. His books are appreciated worldwide. He knows exactly how to write in ways that people can have their needs met.

15. They have mentors, but influencers also mentor many. I have observed a great number of top pediatricians receive various recognitions and awards at the American Academy of Pediatrics meetings. It is very common for the honoree to thank his or her mentors right off the bat in the first few minutes of the acceptance speech.

16. Influencers are superb at marketing their ideas in a way that makes the "buyer" feel good about deciding to buy the

influencer's resources. Robin Sharma, another expert in leadership development, stays in contact with his followers and serves them relentlessly.

17. They endure over time and consistently stay in sync with their destiny and calling. Dr. Cooper from the famous Cooper Clinic in Dallas illustrates this point well. In his eighties he still goes to work and does it with a greater purpose in mind. The Texas Tornado, Dr. DeBakey, did the same thing well into his nineties.

18. Influencers prepare for years. They remind me of one-hundred-meter sprinters—years of hard work for less than ten seconds of performing.

19. Influencers maintain balance. In all areas of their lives they go full out, but not to the detriment of their loved ones. It is great to write books about marriage and fly all over the place, living your passion and doing what makes your heart sing. But how influential are you when you neglect your family? When your spouse decides enough is enough and divorces you, it has the potential to drain your influence.

20. Many are connected to their source. Many times they admit that God made them and that they are not the creators of their many gifts and talents. It makes sense to be thankful to God for our success. Influencers are co creators with a higher power. Jim Rohn and Zig Ziglar—both top motivational speakers and as a result major influencers—were transparent about their faith in a loving God. They did it humbly and sincerely. As a result it generated the respect of their audiences. Very few of their millions and millions of followers were offended.

When I first looked at this list, I wondered, *How is it possible to do all these twenty things all the time?* Then it hit me: these influential people chose their associations with great discernment. Many of them associated with great leaders even when they already were great leaders themselves. In addition, they understood that we are blessed for a bigger purpose. Our progress is not just for ourselves only; it is also meant to serve others. We are meant to bring light. A great teacher, Jesus, once taught thousands on a hill that they are to be salt and light. They were told to never hide their brilliance but to instead influence the world by choosing an attitude of loving kindness.

Our influence on others depends so much on our attitude toward them. When a leader walks into a room and his or her presence commands the room, it may be either due to pride or love. Love is based on a desire to serve others and bring out the best in them. Pride is *demanding* respect. Pride is based upon an enormously inflated ego. Watering the seeds of pride never increases one's influence, yet we all encounter proud people who struggle to learn this key lesson.

Furthermore, if we influence others as their coaches, we make the biggest impact when we are motivated by loving kindness. I always wondered about coaches who influence their teams or individual athletes. I thought, *If a coach teaches a world-class athlete to succeed, how good is the coach at that particular sport? And why is it that so often the coach has never even participated in that sport himself or herself? Or if the coach has participated in that sport, why has the coach not risen to the top if he or she is that good at it?*

I now know the answer. A coach is someone who develops an athlete's talents and potential. These are skills that the athlete does not possess. Coaches are skilled at helping athletes see what they cannot see themselves.

Being influential in our marriages begins with us seeing the potential of another person. It is far easier to move forward together if a wife has a husband who sees potential in her that she does not see in herself and vice versa. As we associate with one another, motivated by bringing out the best, we move forward through both the good and the bad times. Our influence extends beyond the four walls of our homes.

Legacy Leavers

I recently took a test to name the winners over the past ten years of the Super Bowl, Academy Awards, Miss America Pageant, and Nobel Prizes and to name last year's ten wealthiest people in the world. I failed that test.

Then there was another test: name the teacher who influenced you the most, the person who encouraged you as a child, and the person who was your role model in college. I got 100 percent on that test. What is the point?

The point is that none of us remembers all the headlines of the past. The winners of those awards are the best in their fields, yet when the applause dies and the awards get stale, those accolades are soon forgotten.

The people who influence us the most are the ones who *care* about us the most. They live their lives by example. They have invested in our lives. Many continue to do so long after their transition from this physical world.

As Lou Holtz, the famous Notre Dame football coach, said, "When I die my accomplishments will eventually be forgotten. But what I have invested in my players will live on." When I watch my two boys on the football field and I see their caring coaches on the sideline, I cannot help but think of Lou Holtz.

> **When I die my accomplishments will eventually be forgotten. But what I have invested in my players will live on.**
>
> **—Lou Holtz**

Like-Minded Associations

The late Jim Rohn influenced millions around the globe with his books, CDs, and videos. I know of many influential people who have mentioned what a huge impact Rohn had on them. I heard one of these achievers say, "For my car to move I need gasoline, and it also does not move unless I have a Jim Rohn CD in the car." It is a cliché but true that birds of the same feather flock together. Achievers associate with achievers. Like attracts like.

My friend Ron Behrens is an engineer with Chevron. He lives in California, but when he visits my hometown for business, we often get a chance to visit—rarely inside a building but frequently hiking or riding mountain bikes in the Rockies. Ron consistently brings out the best in me because we have so much in common. Whenever we visit, I am always amazed how I lose sense of time. Since we both care about faith, fitness, and family, we never run out of ideas in our conversations. We are

111

like-minded, and our associations, brief as they may be, always end with us already looking forward to the next visit while appreciating the time we had together.

It is the same with my old friend Pierre Nel in South Africa. Pierre and I have remained connected to this day as a result of what we went through in our six years of medical school. We were matched together during anatomy class because our last names were alphabetically close. For a full year we dissected cadavers together. We later studied together, many nights until well after midnight; celebrated our graduation together; and spent many nights on call during our year of internship. We often covered each other's shifts as we discovered together the deep emotions associated with delivering support to suffering patients. I have seen him only four times in thirty years, but we still stay in touch. Recently he sent me an e-mail asking, "How are things on your side of this blue ball?"

He inspires me to always take things to the next level, in part because he always thinks big. In fact, he is not working as a doctor anymore; he now runs an international, multimillion-dollar company in Africa. (Every time I get upgraded to first class I remember what he told me once when I complained about how little space one has in the economy section. He said, "It is time for you to move to the front a bit more often, my friend!")

I have breakfast with a group of like-minded men every Friday. Doing this for the past twenty years has inspired me to always look for ways to move forward. Many of my ideas in this book were tested on this group of men. They have been very patient with me. They endured being the guinea pigs of my one-liners and jokes. And they did this bright and early—long before the sun rose! My association with these men is an association I deeply treasure.

I am blessed to be married to a woman who teaches me more about myself than I can express. A few years ago, I learned a valuable lesson from her. She used to do what most mothers do: care for her kids and in the process forget the inverse golden rule for women, which states, "Do unto yourself what you do unto others." Trying to take better care of her own health, she joined an exercise program called "Bikini Boot Camp." By associating with like-minded women, she is more consistent with her workouts. She finds it harder to exercise on her own—especially when the chilly Canadian climate grips us mercilessly for 60 percent of the year.

> **The Inverse Golden Rule for Women:**
> **Do unto yourself what you do unto others.**

My wife's story shows what happens when we are *intentional* in seeking like-minded associations. However, some like-minded associations often crop up in our lives *unexpectedly*.

One evening, at Cabo San Lucas not so long ago, while getting into a hot tub, I recognized a man's voice from a few years back. I had met the man, Jay, previously in the same hot tub! Jay and four of his friends, all from Minnesota, were there with their wives and a group of boys who recently had graduated from high school. One of the boys was a newly diagnosed diabetic, and this inspired me to ask these men to participate in a marathon to raise money for diabetes. As a result of our association most of us are scheduled to run a marathon in Minneapolis that we now all call "the Event." This unexpected meeting led to all of us moving forward in our abilities to help others.

I am always surprised by how much we have in common with total strangers and how our associations, often unplanned, can bring out the best in others. But then there are times when we encounter people who are not on our wavelength. How can those associations help us move forward?

Other-Minded Associations

John Shaw, a businessman and a good friend from Toronto, said something that resonated with me. He said that people are put in our lives to teach us how to be and also how not to be.

It is a good thing to sometimes move outside all these positive associations. Everyone has a story. We can learn at least one thing from most other people, even the ones who may irritate us at times. I experience this regularly when I travel.

I experience mostly joy when I travel. The only part I rarely enjoy is when security agents do their jobs to keep us safe. I have witnessed a stern agent do his very best to make a most innocent older grandmother appear to be worse than Al Capone! Some of these individuals have tremendous lessons to deliver. There is no doubt that they serve a valuable purpose. Yet I have learned that although they may have power and may perform an important task, their people skills at times can be rudimentary at best. I must quickly add that the majority of security agents do their work in a truly professional manner.

I've gotten many of my best ideas while traveling from cab drivers. They, like barbers, seem to have a wide general knowledge, and they are usually keen to tell you about what they have learned from their clients. Always hungry for life lessons, I am now good at prompting cab drivers to talk about themselves.

Recently in Ottawa, long after midnight, due to a weather-delayed flight, I was driven to my downtown hotel by a cab driver born in the Middle East. I immediately related well to him, and as I listened to his ideas on how to create peace in the Middle East, I realized what an extremely complex and emotional issue with many sides it is. Year by year, it seems to get even *more* complex. Although I did not entirely agree with his opinions, I respected what he had to say and learned a few new ideas.

Often while in the United States for conferences or marathons I get to meet people who feel passionately about the state of the nation. Many say that Canada and the United States essentially have similar cultures. The more I travel in both countries, the more I tend to disagree. These two countries have vastly different ideas about guns, taxation, faith, and the role of government. People from different countries may not always be on the same page, but it is when we associate with diverse cultures that we learn some great lessons.

When I am in the United States and observe very partisan debates, I can always say that a can-do attitude seems to unite Americans. The word *American* ends with *I can*. That can-do attitude can't be any more obvious than in the Apple story. Steve Jobs's life illustrates what I am talking about. Some of us may not be a fan of Apple products, but the company teaches us plenty about the I-can way of delivering technological advances.

Whatever the topic may be—religion, sex, or politics—always try to learn something from those who have different belief systems than your own. The more diverse the culture you live in, the more you can learn from those who are not like-minded. As Dale Carnegie reminded us, when we aim to make friends, the best way to win an argument is to avoid it.

Not all battles are worth fighting; only the ones that are integral to your destiny are worth staying committed to. Strife will ensure that you rarely move forward. It only creates negative energy and confusion. As Dr. Wayne Dyer teaches, when you have to decide between being right or being kind, chose kindness.

When we learn lessons from others, we get enlightened, and as Alan Cohen said so wisely, "Everything looks different in the light." Our perspectives and attitudes are shaped by the company we keep. Choose to associate with high-energy people, but never discount the lessons learned from the way low-energy (not like-minded) individuals conduct themselves.

Writers

Although it is not always possible to be with high-energy friends, it is always possible to learn from high-energy people through their writing. As the Will Rogers quote at the start of the chapter says, we learn by reading. How we read books and allow media to shape us can make a huge impact on our resilience. I am convinced too many people fail to store away resources such as books that will help them prepare for future setbacks. It is important to take time to relax, and for some of us that means watching TV. But what happens when that is all we do and we never open a single book? How does not reading any books impact our health?

Because one of my passions is to eat healthy and help others do the same, I am always browsing through the nutrition section of bookstores. Recently I encountered *The New Abs Diet* by David Zinczenko. I've been told that the cover of a book is the single most influential factor when people decide whether to buy it or not. This book probably stood out because of its bright-orange cover. Zinczenko is editor in chief of *Men's Health*. I have seen him a number of times on the *Today Show*, which is one of NBC's most successful programs. I knew David was witty and charming from watching that show, but after I read the first few pages of this book, I knew it was going to be in my library. Every time I mention this book to my patients, it is almost as if I can see Zinczenko's mischievous smile while making the point of why some foods are really, really loaded with unhealthy fats and sugars. By associating with this author through his books and learning from him, I am able to improve the associations I have with my patients.

Since I help families who struggle to keep their children fit and healthy, I am always curious about why people do what they do in terms of their nutrition and exercise. I remember hearing someone say, "If we know the things we know, then why do we do the things we do?" I believe the answer may lie in us reading a book once and then returning it to the library or a bookshelf and forgetting the timeless truths it delivered to us during a brief season. Someone once reminded me that there are huge benefits to meditating on a book for at least as long as it took us to read it. This person encouraged me to read a book for information, then again for revelation, and finally for application.

For that reason I keep a powerful book, *The Power of Habit* by Charles Duhigg, on my desk where I can review it often. The book addresses how we can change our habits and why we relapse so easily. I have read the book at least three times in order to maintain my own healthy habits. There are a number of other books like this one that I associate with in order to improve myself.

I am also motivated to share appropriate resources with others who may benefit from them. One such book is *Eat Well, Live Well* by Pam Smith. Even though I have never met Pam, I indirectly associate with her when I give medical advice to families. Pam introduced me to what she calls "the Ten Commandments of Great Nutrition":

1. Thou shalt never skip breakfast.
2. Thou shalt eat every three to four hours and have your healthy snack handy.
3. Thou shalt always eat a carbohydrate with a protein.
4. Thou shalt double your fiber.
5. Thou shalt trim the fat from your diet.
6. Thou shalt believe your mother was right: eat your fruits and vegetables.
7. Thou shalt get your vitamins and minerals from food, not pills.
8. Thou shalt drink at least eight glasses of water a day.
9. Thou shalt consume a minimum of sugar, salt, caffeine and alcohol.
10. Thou shalt, never, never go on a fad diet.

Once again, this example shows how books can help us associate with others who have lived their lives by example. Their skills rub off on us because of positive associations. And in turn we pass on information to others we associate with.

One of the joys of reading is that long after the author has transitioned from this physical world into another realm, his or her ideas still are present for our benefit. Recently I was listening to a book on CD while driving down the freeway, and a quote from Robert Frost impacted me so intensely that I had to pull over and write it down: "We all sit in a ring and suppose while the secret sits in the center and knows." Frost, now long gone, still reminds us with his words that the answer we are searching for often is right in front of us.

These are straightforward examples, but here are some practical questions: Which books do you have in your library? How often do you read them? Once you read them, do you intentionally set time aside to meditate on what you found useful? Can you say that you read the most important ones three times—once for information, once for revelation, and once for application?

Great Orators

At a pediatric conference I attended in Chicago I had the honor to hear a speech by the surgeon general at that time, Dr. Regina M. Benjamin. It brought the audience of pediatricians to their feet, and here is why.

She eloquently shared a story of when she worked as a family doctor and got a call from a patient in serious pain one Saturday morning. The patient was a janitor at a school and needed a stronger pain-killer just to function. Dr. Benjamin prescribed some medication with instructions that the patient was to see her for follow-up in forty-eight hours.

Two days later the patient was there but still in significant pain. When asked what happened, she answered, "I could not afford the medication." Dr. Benjamin felt bad for her patient and offered to pay for the medication out of her own pocket. This embarrassing situation ended on a positive note when the patient insisted on paying Dr. Benjamin back, thus restoring her lost pride. But Dr. Benjamin's point was that there are hardworking people who cannot always afford health care that some people take for granted. She had entered public health to make a difference not to her own patients but to millions.

In the same speech she also mentioned one of her favorite leadership styles: leadership from behind. In this style we reach behind us and pull others forward, telling them they have what it takes, setting an example they can follow, and reassuring them with affirmations such as "Go ahead … I have your back covered." What a way to leave a legacy and, through your associations, touch the future.

I also remember sitting in an audience of over five thousand people in the Moscone Convention Center in San Francisco. It was the first time in my life that I saw an audience give a standing ovation to the speaker, in this case General Colin Powell, before he even ascended to the podium. He did not disappoint us and passionately delivered a profoundly powerful message entitled "America's Promise." I learned that day that his passion was to help young people succeed. People who associated with this retired general could not help but be passionate themselves. Colin Powell taught me what can happen when we do things with consistent commitment and enthusiasm.

When we intentionally watch great speakers, our associations, like a plane just after takeoff, take us to a higher altitude. We move forward.

Media

There should be no doubt that we become who we are in part due to who we associate with. If it is true that many of us spend endless hours—almost the whole evening—watching TV or surfing the Internet, could it be that our media associations can make us both better and worse? And could the impact of excessive media use be *particularly* negative for children whose brains are still under construction?

Dr. Michael Rich calls himself a "mediatrician," a pediatrician who knows a lot about how media impacts young people. He works at Harvard and is the catalyst behind a great resource on the issue of how media impacts families: www.cmch.tv. Any parent who wants to know more about media's impact on our children should bookmark this superb site. Dr. Rich reminds us that although there are mostly negative outcomes as a result of our excessive associations with media, there is also the potential to intentionally seek out positive media.

I used to watch morning television shows such as *Good Morning America* and the *Today Show* almost every day. Now, in order to save time, I never watch them live. I instead always watch a few days after recording them so that way I can flash through ads and skip news that is not news anymore because it has already sorted itself out by the time I am watching the show. Not infrequently, these programs inform and entertain me, and it pays off later. I get new ideas, such as which books to read, websites to research, and information to share on my blogs and in newspaper columns.

Many of these ideas also come in handy when I do TV interviews as a regular contributor regarding health issues and trends. The media work I do every week informs and energizes me; my associations with positive media enable me to contribute wisely in a consistent manner.

But it is not always about *me* contributing to media; it is about those I associate with. To illustrate allow me to tell you about my friend Dave Kelly, who used to anchor a popular local morning show many years ago. When we did interviews for morning TV, we always seemed to be on the same page—Dave, like me, has a habit of always being curious. As a result he discovered that I am a marathon runner. I finally succeeded in convincing Dave to join me for one of my many marathons. It was a lot of fun.

Dave has a great sense of humor. At one point in the race we passed through many intersections with only green lights, no reds for mile after mile. Dave leaned over to me and said, "It's good all the lights are green, because we will finish faster!" We laughed together and thanked the police offers who selflessly controlled the flow of traffic so as to give the marathoners preference. Being with Dave always means that there is a high likelihood of humor. My associations with Dave have enabled me to move closer to reaching my potential as a regular part-time medical contributor to various TV shows.

TV has the ability to entertain and inform, although some would argue over the quality of the media we associate with. Sometimes people say, "I avoid newspapers. They focus on the negative." I tend to disagree, and to illustrate, I recently read a story about the history of beards in Russia. It may be trivial, but it shows how reading the "right" articles in newspapers can be entertaining at times and make for great water-cooler talks!

On September 5, 1698, Peter the Great slapped a tax on beards. Czar Peter had an aversion to beards, so he required men with beards to pay one hundred rubles if they wanted to go unshaven. Proof of payment was a metal token inscribed with a beard on one side and the words "The beard is a superfluous burden."

We often think of media in terms of superficial entertainment. It is true, but how about paying closer attention to the media you associate with? Choose the right media, articles and clips that increase your energy level. There are indeed higher-energy media resources we can align with, as opposed to media marked by violence, profanity, and ego-dominant programs that give this industry a negative reputation.

I shall never forget seeing the influential media personality Fred Rogers, give a keynote speech in front of five thousand pediatricians. Fred Rogers, known as Mr. Rogers, produced a popular TV show for children on PBS. He always made a point of using TV to teach young kids universally accepted values like respect, honesty, and courage. I was honored to observe this gentle, kind man at a conference in San Francisco where he spoke to a group that often is skeptical about media. I shall always remember the moment when he was presented with a baseball jacket, featuring the logo of the American Academy of Pediatrics on it. He promptly took off his own jacket and put on his new gift, doing up its zipper. With a wide grin on his face, Mr. Rogers proclaimed, "It's a beautiful day in the neighborhood!"

Organizations

There are three organizations that have deeply impacted me: Dale Carnegie Training, the American Academy of Pediatrics (AAP), and the Canadian Pediatric Society (CPS).

I used to be a part-time instructor for Carnegie Training. I cannot say enough about the value this organization added to my life. If it was not for Carnegie, I would not have been able to do all the media work I do in front of TV cameras or on radio. Prior to taking the training I was normal, meaning I belonged to the *majority* of people who were more fearful of public speaking than death itself! My association with the Dale Carnegie resources enables me today to talk to crowds of any size without an ounce of fear.

One of my mentors is John Fisher, the former owner of the Carnegie franchise in Western Canada. John and his wife, Faye, taught me many lessons over the years, but the bottom line is that whenever I associate with them, I am encouraged to do what they do so well: always talk in terms of the other person's interest and become a better listener.

As the president of the Alberta chapter of the AAP, I have had the honor to meet various leaders in this dynamic organization. They have taught me much about looking after the health of children and also about ways to set priorities. My association with the AAP has confirmed to me that maintaining a dynamic approach to getting things done all hinges on great leadership and the ability to prioritize wisely. I plan to keep this association alive for many years to come.

My association with the Canadian Pediatric Society has involved mainly committee work. As a member of their psychosocial committee, I had the honor to author the society's original three papers on children and media, literacy, and effective discipline. This association with the CPS taught me how to deal with controversial topics and to work as a team with others who sometimes bordered on the absurd with their criticism of these papers. It has been said that not a single poem has been written by a committee. I found this to be true while serving on committees with well-meaning but, at times, overly critical peers. From this experience I learned that when I give feedback to others, I should start with what is right rather than what is wrong. My association with the CPS also allowed me to develop new skills when dealing with media because the society asked me to represent them when there were media inquiries on these three topics.

So many times organizations allow us to learn two things about ourselves as we serve others: our strengths and weaknesses. These associations help us move closer to living our lives on purpose and in the service of others. We move forward daily.

Faith Followers

One of the people I associate with regularly is a man who officiated at my wedding two decades ago. He still teaches me fresh insights on many a Sunday. I am talking about my pastor, Dr. Len Zoeteman. The way Len explains how faith works and how to grow in that area is second to none. When I get to listen to this wise man, I always make sure that my fountain pen is filled to capacity with fresh ink and that my journal is close by.

I also like to carry with me some key points he has made. I keep these brief notes in the shirt pocket close to my heart—laminated and to be reviewed often, especially when I am caught in long, slow-moving lines. As I mentioned earlier, influencers rarely waste time. I apply this principle when I am tempted to complain about, once again, being in the slowest lane. This habit gives me the opportunity to learn and memorize timeless truths explained by Len, a man I feel blessed to learn from.

One time I was in a busy, noisy mall on a Friday night. I was disturbed by the consumerism and seeing young people mesmerized by the magnetic draw of the latest technology. People were frantically competing for their material desires. Unexpectedly, I met Len and his wife. His charismatic presence immediately re-energized me in minutes. His grounded, higher energy elevated my own energy. I shall never forget that simple lesson of how our associations can help us move forward.

Over the years my list of spiritual mentors has grown. Although many of us have mentors in the areas of career, sports, fashion, psychology, philosophy, and various other areas driven by contemporary culture, I believe it is also important to go beyond the physical realm. It is important to have spiritual mentors we associate with regularly.

It has been said that if in all we say, do, and think we are motivated by the force of love, we will live a lives worth living. For that reason I often imagine my spiritual mentors—both those still alive and those who have already transitioned from us—as passengers in my car, visitors in my home, observers in my clinic, or fellow runners alongside me during marathons. I simply *imagine* them keeping me accountable, watching me, and giving me feedback. I often meditate on how they would have expressed love if they had faced the same challenges I face.

Some spiritual mentors are like actors in a movie or play; they are on our stage or screen but for a moment. Others are the main players and stay much longer in order to teach and inspire us as we continue to expand our awareness. These mentors are more than consultants or gurus; they are heaven-sent souls synchronistically placed on our paths to help us reach a grounded state. Being fully grounded is the ultimate motive for deciding to become more spiritual.

Many of my patients are Jewish. A few years ago a cantor, Alex Stein, whose children were patients of mine, decided to relocate to Toronto. He was good friends with Marvin Hamlisch, the iconic composer and musician known throughout the world. I was privileged to be invited to a concert by Hamlisch and Stein, and although I am not a member at the synagogue, Alex Stein made me feel at home. It was a true honor to associate with such a kind cantor. I learned the value of transcending religion and experiencing the only motive for faith, which is more compassion, love, and contentment. Even thousands of years ago, long before the current era of new spirituality, the Talmud, a Jewish book filled with timeless wisdom, said, "Who is rich? He who is content." When we associate with those who value spirituality, often we end up being wiser and thus more content. But what about those of us who are turned off by divisive religious traditions?

It is important to remember that regardless of the spiritual tradition we subscribe to, in the end we all came from one single source. Einstein explained it well when he was questioned about why various religions seem to be at odds with each other at times: "All religions, arts and sciences are branches of the same tree. All these aspirations are directed toward ennobling man's life, lifting it from the sphere of mere physical existence and leading the individual towards freedom."

Sometimes all we need to do is to forget for a moment about all the above associations and how they may help us grow. We need to balance the serious with some play and head down to an Irish pub. You do not need to order a pint of Guinness if you are not inclined toward consuming any alcohol. But keep your eyes open, as I did, and see if the pub has this saying on the wall:

An Irish Friendship Wish

May there always be work for your hands to do;
May your purse always hold a coin or two;
May the sun always shine on your windowpane;
May a rainbow be certain to follow each rain;

May the hand of a friend always be near you;
May God fill your heart with gladness to cheer you.
And may you be in heaven a half hour before the devil knows you're dead.

This simple poem reminds us that that our associations with true friends are invaluable in our journey forward. The poem mentions God and the devil, and in the next chapter I shall explore what it means to have a heart filled with God.

Action Steps

1. *Take the time to consistently sit down and list the people who always leave you inspired and motivated.* Do it at least once a week. Never take these people for granted. Be *grateful* for their presence in your life. They are teachers sent to you at the right time—when you are ready to learn and grow.

2. *It may not always be possible to be in their physical presence, but if they have written books or websites, associate with them through those resources.* I find it useful during some of my runs to listen to the teachings of men and women I respect. Not only do I exercise my physical muscles, but I also strengthen my faith and my mind by associating with people who value living life positively each and every day.

3. *Search out experts who walk the talk.* There are a lot of experts out there, but not all of them walk the talk. They may have written books on wellness, but they don't exercise consistently and are inconsistent with their eating patterns. They may be experts in how to get along with others, but they are divorced numerous times.

4. *Associate with people who understand the value of having the right attitudes, opinions, and outlooks.* Check their dispositions carefully before you invest time with them. Notice how they respond to difficulties, what temperaments they have, what tendencies and mannerisms they cultivate, what their most consistent mind frames are, and what kind of inclinations they consistently exhibit.

5. *If you don't like your beliefs, expectations, words, and thoughts, check your associations carefully again and again.* Then make the necessary changes. What you think, believe, and speak depends so much on whom you associate with.

6. *If you find yourself in a situation where you cannot avoid being with negative individuals, then be a positive role model to them.* Try to help them to grow, improve, and be stronger. Learn from them anyhow. Remember that Christ taught, "Love your enemies." Accept them instead of judging them.

7. *Take the time to encourage and thank those who inspire you the most.* Even the most famous and influential people are human; they enjoy hearing from those who appreciate how they live their lives as worthy role models. They may keep a simple handwritten note for years to come. Perhaps that note may end up on a wall somewhere framed to serve as an object of encouragement. Even influential people have their down moments. It may be that your note of thanks can brighten your role model's day.

CHAPTER 6

FAITH

Faith can always overcome fear. Faith is the one power against which fear cannot stand. Master faith and you will automatically master fear.
—Dr. Norman Vincent Peale

I keep *The Power of Positive Thinking*, one of my favorite books, right by my bedside table. I try to read a page or two every night before I go to sleep. That way my subconscious mind is filled with the positive. I also make it a habit to take the book with me wherever I travel anywhere in the world.

In fact, as I type these words at the Frankfurt Airport, waiting to get my next flight to South Africa, the book is in my briefcase. It already reminded me earlier today, while I was meditating in the reclined seat of a jetliner at dawn, high above the Atlantic Ocean, that positive faith brings positive results.

I have read numerous books about the importance of cultivating right thinking, but I *always* return to this book for its timeless wisdom and insights because few other books explain the power of our thoughts better. Its author, Dr. Peale, is a pioneer who wrote many decades ago about concepts that are dressed up today as new. Dr. Peale was far ahead of his time. His writings are *still* contemporary today.

The book originally was called *The Power of Positive Faith*. Editors, however, changed the title so it would resonate with more readers. I have a habit of copying a few sentences from any book I read and then using that as a bookmark. One of those bookmarks originating from Dr. Peale's book says, "Faith is the most powerful of all forces operating in humanity and when you have it in depth nothing can get you down."

For many of us there have been times when we felt so down we could see no way out. The pain and sorrow of our situation may have felt as if we were stuck at the bottom of a deep, dark pit where nobody could hear our desperate pleading for help. What caused us to be in this place may vary, but all these situations have one thing in common: we somehow got through it and moved forward. The question is how we moved forward—in bitterness or in faith, in fear or in love? How did we make our choices? My wife and I, over the past year, had to answer these very questions.

The Darkest Chapters Can Bring Light

It has been said that life is a string of lessons, one after another. Reading or hearing about these lessons is one thing, but *experiencing* them firsthand provides a time of profound growth. After decades of living a rather uncomplicated life, my wife and I were about to learn one of the biggest lessons ever. Together, we were about to enter one of the darkest chapters in our lives.

About a year ago my wife lost consciousness for minutes due to her heart suddenly malfunctioning. I was not present, but my son Jonathan was in the same room. Jon rushed downstairs to get me and calmly said, "Dad, you better come upstairs quickly. Mom does not look very good …" When I entered our study, I found Corinne lifeless.

I struggled to identify the occasional, faint pulse. She was unconscious. While waiting for help to arrive after we called 911, all I could do was to believe, with *all* the faith I had, that she would not die but would return to us. She survived that terrible trial delivered to us without any warning but unfortunately experienced two more similar events.

The final event took place during a spring break as a family. We were having fun together during a Caribbean cruise when Corinne experienced yet another spell, this time marked by her having fixed dilated pupils. She was completely unresponsive. I thought her life was over. Again, I had to choose between faith and fear at that moment. She survived.

> **We were having fun together during a Caribbean cruise when Corinne experienced yet another spell, this time marked by her having fixed dilated pupils. I thought her life was over.**

Doctors were stumped, completely clueless as to why her heart was causing blackouts. We were told that she recovered because her body produced its own adrenaline, which started the heart again. Corinne and I both are physicians, so we know that doctors are human; even the best among us at times cannot make a diagnosis.

As a doctor I have also learned over the years that we can do a great job of stitching up a gaping wound. The healing process takes over once the physician places the final stitch, and the science of wound healing kicks in and continues, independent of our opinions as doctors. Just as a farmer plants seeds, there comes a moment when an unseen force intelligently takes over. Healing and growth progress on time and on purpose—regardless of our religions, philosophies, and dogmas. The healing wound does not care if we believe in God ... it heals anyhow. A rose opens up anyhow. The sun rises anyhow. The body, well crafted, functions anyhow, even before Nobel Prize winners discovered its stunning innate wisdom.

Corinne was not in the care of Nobel winners, but we were blessed to meet with diligent men and women trying to figure it all out. These clinicians relied on an implanted device, a loop monitor, which diagnosed why her heart can suddenly stop functioning. Her condition is labeled polymorphic ventricular tachycardia or torsades de pointes.

Since then she has been fitted with a pacemaker and defibrillator. This will be so for the rest of her life, but we face our future with a deeper faith. In spite of a fatal, formerly undiagnosed heart condition, she is alive today. Our faith enabled us to find hope in our darkest days.

We've learned from experience that things that are impossible with humans are possible with God. We experienced a force and intelligence beyond our understanding—a force who delivers peace that permeates every cell of our bodies as long as our hearts remain receptive. We also learned much about situations where too many coincidences cannot be explained anymore as coincidences.

I do not have the faith to say that these events were mere coincidences. These events were *major* misfortunes … *one after another.* It was not a bruise, a fracture, or an infection resolved easily with the right antibiotic— it was a serious matter of life and death. My four kids nearly lost a mother, and I could have been without my wife and best friend. I now see that when our time is not up, it is not up. Indeed there is a higher power, far greater than us, consistently at work. There are no accidents. In fact, to illustrate the perfect timing of God, soon after my wife's discharge from the hospital we spotted a dozen kindergarten students crossing a very busy avenue led by a loving leader. All the children were holding on to the same rope. The symbolism of being led by someone far wiser than us, holding on to a rope by faith, and thus getting through danger safely was not lost on me at that moment. Our leader loves us, far more than we realize.

This dramatic misfortune made me more aware of how the God of the universe loves us. For example, whenever I pass the chair where I first found Corinne lifeless, I remind myself that we both are *deeply* loved by our creator. In fact, as I type these words, I am looking at that very chair. I rarely look at the chair without thanking God for second opportunities to move forward. I intentionally pause a bit longer and bring my palms together, holding them close to my own heart.

When I meditate in the mornings in the study, the same room where she collapsed, I remember also how doctors told us at one point that her heart situation was not fatal. Meanwhile, it *was* potentially fatal, yet she survived. More than once, we saw the face of death, but she was kept alive to remain with us longer and fulfill her purpose. After the first event, a mentor I deeply respect told us it would not happen again. But it *did* happen again and again. It happened again and again not because we lacked faith but because it was a way to teach us a lesson, which is that we are not in control. A higher intelligence is.

I've always cultivated a strong faith, but now I experience an *inner* knowing of God's control, love, and provision. It is one thing to intellectually buy into the notion that we have a source; it is something completely different to *experience* the love of that source. This experience is vastly different from being conditioned by a religious culture where so often the main focus is on rules and rituals—as opposed to love.

My personal experience of hardships taught me valuable lessons about faith. It has been said that pain pushes and vision pulls. I have been both pulled and pushed to a *higher* awareness. I know now that a divine power controls it *all*. When we think we have the power to operate our faith the same way we operate a vending machine, as if we control it all, we are sorely mistaken. God is not an ATM or a vending machine dispensing what we want at our command. But if God is not an ATM, what do others have to say about God? How do others define faith?

Faith—Defined by Influential Souls

The following quote by Thomas Aquinas explains the mind-sets of those who are skeptical about faith: "To one who has faith, no explanation is necessary. To one without faith, no explanation is possible." Some people have already decided no explanation of faith will suffice; not even the words of people they respect will change their views of faith. In writing this chapter, I decided to research the views on faith as expressed by a wide variety of highly respected individuals.

One such person is Ayn Rand, known for developing a philosophical system she called objectivism. Ayn Rand believed that God is a being whose only definition is that he is beyond man's power to conceive. I could not agree more and find it disturbing when some people claim, with great confidence, their ability to *fully* understand the creator of the universe. Those who tell us they can fathom God are ignoring scriptures, for the Bible says that God's judgments are unfathomable and unsearchable. We can never know God's mind, and we cannot understand His thoughts or become His counselor (Romans 11:33–34). God may be unfathomable according to the Bible, but I always remind myself at the same time that God's nature is love. If the Bible tells me that God is unfathomable but that He is love, what then do other influential observers have to say about faith?

The explanations and opinions of influential men like Khalil Gibran, Martin Luther King Jr., Albert Einstein, Voltaire, St. Augustine, and Victor Hugo have impacted my own views of faith profoundly. I reviewed my personal journal not so long ago and rediscovered what I consider to be thoughtful definitions of faith as expressed by well-known individuals:

- "Faith is to believe what you do not see; the reward of this faith is to see what you believe." (Saint Augustine)
- "Faith consists in believing when it is beyond the power of reason to believe." (Voltaire)
- "Faith is a knowledge within the heart, beyond the reach of proof." (Khalil Gibran)
- "Faith is passionate intuition." (William Wordsworth)
- "Faith is the bird that feels the light when the dawn is still dark." (Rabindranath Tagore)
- "The only faith that wears well and holds its color in all weathers is that which is woven of conviction and set with the sharp mordant of experience." (James Russell Lowell)
- "To me faith means not worrying." (John Dewey)
- "Keep your faith in God, but keep your powder dry." (Oliver Cromwell)
- "My reason nourishes my faith and my faith my reason." (Norman Cousins)
- "Vision looks upward and becomes faith." (Stephen Samuel Wise)
- "Let faith be the bridge to overcome evil and welcome good." (Maya Angelou)

When asked what God meant to him, Albert Einstein, one of the world's most intelligent human beings, answered, "That deep emotional conviction of the presence of a superior reasoning power, which is revealed in the incomprehensible universe, forms my idea of God." Einstein, a human with superior reasoning power, discovered that we live in an incomprehensible universe. Being aware of his own superior reasoning power, Einstein also understood that there is a presence of another force, a force with a far *superior* reasoning than himself.

We may be inspired by the way in which these great intellectuals expressed their understanding of faith, but at some point in all our lives we decide how we will allow our level of faith to determine what we believe, what we expect, what we say, and what we think. Let me illustrate with a word picture.

The following word picture of faith from Martin Luther King Jr. really resonates with my soul: "Faith is taking the first step even when you don't see the whole staircase. Take the first step in faith. You don't have to see the whole staircase, just take the first step." We can choose to never take that first step. Or we can choose to move forward and, by faith, take that very first step.

> **Faith is taking the first step even when you don't see the whole staircase. Take the first step in faith. You don't have to see the whole staircase, just take the first step.**
> **—Martin Luther King Jr.**

This capacity to choose is one of the most valuable faculties given to us. We have complete freedom to choose whatever we want to believe. But ultimately those choices determine our lives. They determine our daily thought patterns. We become what we think, and when we change our thoughts, we change our lives.

My Personal Definition of Faith

My definition of faith is simply a trust and knowing that there are no coincidences. Faith is all about a deep personal trust in the love and intelligence of the creator, regardless of circumstances. When we experience the great provider in matters such as life and death, we get to a place of inner knowing. For many this becomes a quantum moment, a moment where we experience a profound enlightenment. We move from the logical intellect to an almost-mystical, deep, inner awareness.

This trust in a power far wiser than us makes us spiritual. To be spiritual means to be grounded at all times and under all circumstances. Spirituality allows us to experience the sacred in such a way that we become independent of religion's rigid rules. Instead we experience a new way of living and attain a spiritual awareness of life and peace—not just life, but abundant life to the overflow. By trusting fully and not trying to figure everything out at all times, we learn what it means to surrender to a higher intelligence. Instead of trying to find the answers to the many why questions, we focus on God's provision during times of desperate darkness. It means that we move into a new state of being. I call this transformation. We are transformed once we find out how faith defeats fear. We are transformed when we discover that fear and love cannot coexist. Like a caterpillar transforms into a butterfly, there is no way to return to the former self.

The Benefits of Faith

I have observed that those who *apply* their faith experience a greater inner strength, have more resilience, and endure longer. They feel a burden drop off their backs when they ask their creator for support, and they control their anxieties better. They develop powers within themselves they never knew they had. They have a complete calmness that inspires others. They handle their struggles with courage and never lose hope.

Adversity

In my clinic I see people go through challenges every day. It has been my honor over the past three decades to be there with them, in the same room, listening to their pain and suffering. It stirs one's soul to see the faces of those going through suffering, pain, and loss. But I have observed that three factors always seem to sustain them in their struggles: family, friends, and faith. For many, a firm faith foundation enables them to overcome their sudden storms.

In the chapter on adversity I mentioned how others can energize us and help us cope with calamities much better than we can cope alone. I can honestly say that my patients who relied on family, friends, and faith ultimately did the best. Not only did they manage to move forward during dark times, but they also continued to move forward years later. They were able to transform the *struggle* in their lives into the *message* of their lives.

Another example of someone who transformed a major adversity into a powerful message is Rick Warren, who went through a dark chapter when his son committed suicide. Rick said, "I do not need answers to my questions. It will not bring my son back. What I need is God." Despite this devastating loss he has remained grounded, but perhaps more importantly, his own peace allows him to continue his teaching at a much higher level. He got pruned. He now produces more fruit than ever. Millions resonate with his authentic wisdom every week. He has over a million followers on Twitter and inspires many daily with his strong faith.

Adversities test our faith and can bring us closer to God. The atrocities that took place during the Holocaust tested the faith of many. One such person who survived persecution and racism, Elie Wiesel, wrote, "I have not lost faith in God. I have moments of anger and protest. Sometimes I've been closer to him for that reason."

> **I have not lost faith in God. I have moments of anger and protest. Sometimes I've been closer to him for that reason.**
> **—Elie Wiesel**

During these moments when we sense our close alignment with God, we may wonder if it is possible to overcome all things with God's help. All my life I have been taught that with God all things are possible. I think what that means is that with God we are empowered to rise *above* our suffering. I do not believe that with God's help *all* things are possible. For example, even with faith in God I cannot run the one hundred meters at the next Olympics at age sixty and win the gold medal; with God's help I also cannot dribble a football. All things may not be possible, but a reliance on a power far greater than ourselves can help us handle hardships.

Whenever I see an image of an eagle, I am reminded of how they handle their own struggles: they lock their wings, surrender to the strong winds, and soar to an altitude where there is a definite quietness. They trust their instinct. They have faith in their inner wisdom. They align themselves with the forces of nature. No wonder I once heard someone say, "Have eagle faith—faith where you lock your wings and ride out storms; you soar."

Serenity

One of the main benefits of a foundation of faith is serenity. Serenity is a sure sense of being fully grounded. I see evidence of this on the faces of spiritual people, and it is reflected in the calm confidence of their voices. They appear to be at ease, fully present in the moment and not anxious at all about the future. They have an inner *knowing* that there is a creator of the universe who never abandons the creation. Calamities may try to create confusion, but faith sustains them. They are at peace even when calamities try to obstruct their progress.

Horatio Spafford, a lawyer who lived in the nineteenth century, is one of the most inspiring examples to me of someone whose faith sustained him through serious setbacks In his life Spafford encountered a number of losses. His only son died. His business burnt down. The economy disintegrated, forcing his career into a sudden halt. While he remained in Chicago to deal with these challenges, his wife and four daughters set sail for Europe, where he was to meet them at a later date, but their ship sunk. All four children died. Faith in God sustained him through these losses. He did not become bitter. Instead he penned these words:

> When peace, like a river, attendeth my way,
> When sorrows like sea billows roll.
> Whatever my lot, Thou has taught me to say,
> It is well, it is well with my soul.

Spafford's experience teaches us that aligning with faith-filled, spiritual living inspires us to a place of total peace and surrender whatever our lot may be.

My own definition of serenity is when we experience a sense of inner peace regardless of going through pain. Such a serene sense of inner peace flooded my soul the night I flew back from Africa after watching my dad take his last breath. I sensed his spirit departed from his body, which lay there, destroyed by pancreatic cancer. On that flight back, just before we landed at Heathrow Airport in London, these words uttered by B. C. Forbes made total sense to me: "He who has faith has an inward reservoir of courage, hope, confidence, calmness and assuring trust that all will come out well—even though to the world it may appear to come out mostly badly." By the time my family met me at the airport in Canada I *knew* that all would come out well. My faith sustains me each and every moment I miss my dad. I am serene because I know I will see him again one day.

Hope

Another benefit of real spirituality is hope. Thomas Aquinas said that faith has to do with things that are not seen and hope with things that are not at hand. When we understand that faith deals with the unseen, we will move forward, believing that such a faith will help us develop powers within ourselves that we never knew we already had.

When the negative circumstances of life move in like clouds on a sunny day, we still know that the sun is shining above the clouds. We do not lose our hope that the sun will manifest at the right time. When Joel Osteen was accused of telling people to have too much hope, he answered, "It is too late to convince me that faith does not work. There are too many examples in my life of where it worked."

Faith indeed fuels our hope, especially when we hold on to our God-given inner strength and continue to expect the best while leaving the outcome to a higher power.

> **Faith will help us develop powers within ourselves which we never knew we already had.**

Respect for Creation

Although I appreciate that not everyone believes they were created by a higher power, once I completed medical school, I could not help but be in awe of how wonderfully the body functions when it functions in health. Hard as I may try, I am unable to believe that our amazing bodies can function well without a creator's input. I do not know who else could have thought of creating a living being over nine months so complex, so wonderfully made.

Any doctor who is at the top of his or her field knows a lot about pathology, physiology, and the latest scientific facts about the body. But how do they explain the intricate ways in which the body functions—ways that are still being discovered and endlessly explored? We will never get to a place where we know all we need to know about how marvelously the body is assembled.

In one of his brilliant books Dr. Joe Dispenza talks about an intelligence who is far greater than us. As a physician I trust this intelligence myself and invite you to meditate on these words written by Dr. Dispenza:

Call it what you will but this is the universal intelligence that's giving you life right now. It organizes and orchestrates the hundreds of thousands of notes in the harmonious symphony that is your physiology—those things that are part of your autonomic nervous system. This intelligence keeps your heart beating more than 101,000 times a day to pump more than two gallons of blood per minute, travelling more than 60, 000 miles in each 24-hour period. As you finish reading this sentence, your body will have made 25 trillion cells. And each of the 70 trillion cells that make up your body execute somewhere between 100,000 to 6 trillion functions per second. You will inhale 2 million liters of oxygen today, and each time you inhale, that oxygen will be distributed to every cell in your body within seconds.

Do you consciously keep track of all that? Or does something that has a mind so much greater than your mind, and a will so much greater than your will, do it for you? That's love. In fact, that intelligence loves you so much that it loves you into life. This invisible field of intelligence exists beyond space and time, and it's where all things material come from.

I am convinced that all of us were created for a purpose and that the creator has stored within our minds and our personalities tremendous potential and strength that enables us to always get better and better—to move forward if we choose to do so.

When I reflect on the creation of influential people, I think of how a higher power enables many Nobel Prize winners and Olympic athletes to excel. I personally do not have the faith to believe that all these success stories exist independent of a source. Is it really plausible that all of it hinge on coincidence after coincidence randomly unfolding one after another?

Freedom

Many believe with their heads. This is an intellectual faith. However, real spirituality is when we get to a place of inner knowing. This knowing sets us free from fears, anxieties, and negative thinking. We are set free because we trust in the unseen. Though we cannot see electricity, we still believe and trust it fully; the same can be said about us trusting any electronic device when we press its buttons but cannot fully explain how it operates so flawlessly. Just like electricity, God is unseen, and when our spirituality brings us in closer alignment with our source, we develop a deeper trust.

Theologians refer to God as being omnipresent because God is spirit, unhindered by physical limitations, and this spirit is love. We can stop fretting once we realize that God is omnipresent and that we are loved by the source of the universe. Once we choose to meditate on this love, we become aware that we are never alone or separated from God—even when we allow our egos to get in the way. Love walks beside us, and there is nowhere we can go where we are without the care of our creator.

As our faith increases, we will develop a growing confidence and trust that things will unfold as they should. Many spiritual teachers, as they look back over their lives, can clearly see how God allowed the right people and the right events to unfold on purpose, directing their paths. In fact, that is the summary of Wayne Dyer's book *I Can See Clearly Now*.

When we become partners with this higher power, we align with a force who allows us to experience more supernatural living. I like this definition of the supernatural explained to me once: it is when your *natural* is combined with His *super*. We do our part to the best of our abilities, but at the same time we surrender by letting go and allowing God to be God—even when we do not fully understand Him. This surrender sets us free from having to try so hard all the time. (There is no point calling God a higher power if we fully understood Him. Remember Einstein referred to God as "the presence of a superior reasoning power.")

Creativity

Faith also contributes to our creativity. When the composer Joseph Haydn was asked how he was able to be so creative, he said, "When I decide to compose I pray and thank God that it has been accomplished. Then I do it. If it doesn't come the first time, I pray again. Then it comes." I have found this to be true numerous times when writing my monthly medical columns for one of Canada's largest newspapers, the *Calgary Herald*.

Not so long ago I read about an author who kept a picture of his spiritual mentor by the desk where he wrote. He used positive imaging to "see" the face of his kind teacher watching him craft his profession. As a result words started to flow effortlessly and so profusely that writer's block never seemed possible. Once again I have found the same to be true when I keep on the desk where I write a picture of my most influential mentor, a mentor who has authored numerous *New York Times* best-selling books on faith.

Developing Your Faith

Faith and fitness have this one thing in common: they both take time to develop. Faith is not simply a matter of suddenly grasping all truths. It is something that takes time to grow. Seeing one's faith grow requires patience, but the payoff is huge considering all the benefits I mentioned previously. Mahatma Gandhi reminded us that patience is worth developing and must endure to the end of time. He also noted that a living faith will last in the midst of the blackest storm. We gain this living faith that will outlast our blackest storms when we are faithful in small things. As mentioned in a previous chapter, consistency is the fine line separating success and failure. To become full of faith we choose to be *consistently* faithful.

I once looked at my fading tan lines a few days after returning from a sunny vacation. It struck me that if there is no sun, a tan fades really fast, and that is the same analogy with faith. We may see the value of spirituality, but if we stop developing it, it will fade fast. Similarly when we have a broken leg and a muscle is not put to use, it becomes atrophied in a cast. The development of our faith has to be intentional.

So how does one develop faith? I am sure the list may look very different for each of us, but my experience in my various roles as a doctor, husband, father, and athlete has provided me with these observations:

1. Believe that it is possible to increase in faith just as you believe you can increase in knowledge. Faith either grows or shrinks. It cannot stay static. Plato said, "We are twice armed if we fight with faith." Life is a battle to overcome obstacles, one after another, and it is a good idea to be "twice armed." Faith sustains us during our seemingly endless struggles.

2. Expect new revelations daily. You are never too old to grow.

3. Affirm only words of faith. Remain committed to this habit.

4. Discipline your thoughts daily.

5. Expose yourself to spiritual writings, and keep an open mind. We all will have different methods of fueling our faith. I respect the many truths in various scriptures and often remind myself that they all say the same thing in two words: "Love more." Personally, the Bible continues to inspire me daily; it helps my faith to expand.

6. Expose yourself to people whose passion is to develop faith in others.

7. Do not confuse faith with religion. Religion is about rules; faith is about results. If you want results from your faith, do not confuse it with religion.

Faith versus Religion

Faith is not to be confused with organized religion. This is not a chapter about organized, dogmatic, traditional religion, which seems to have become more and more irrelevant to those who sincerely are searching for deeper relationships with their creator. This is a chapter to help you move forward by considering the benefits of aligning with the creator of the universe.

It is my humble experience that the kindest and nicest people one can ever meet today have zero interest in religion. Why? Because various denominational traditions not only offend spiritual seekers but also make them feel unloved, unappreciated, judged, and nonrelevant. The self-righteous attitude that marks some religions can become abrasive, and it has been written that to be abrasive is to be nonpersuasive.

What some see in religion they find utterly useless and hypocritical. To them religion can be impractical, too traditional, divisive, selfish, strife-driven, too egotistical, and simply a waste of time and energy. Who can blame those who rejected their faith after growing up in a place of worship where rules and regulations trumped relationships? Real faith is rooted in one single truth: love.

The great teacher, Christ, taught that to whom much is given, from them much is expected. He desired for his followers to serve other the way he did. In fact, to demonstrate he stooped down and washed the dirty feet of his followers. This action requires a sensitivity to care for people we meet day by day and also to care for those we have never met. The core message of faith is that we should care for others and not use faith to benefit us only.

Well-known author and speaker Tony Campolo, who refers to himself as a "passionate follower of Christ," recently spoke in Calgary. During an interview with the local newspaper, Campolo called the theology of self-interest "idiotic."

He was in Calgary as a guest of World Vision, an organization I teamed up with to raise money through marathon running to help feed starving children anywhere on the planet. Although Tony is a Christian, one can apply the following quote from the local newspaper to anyone who has made spirituality a priority: "I have to break out of the idea that God only wants to bless me. God is calling me to look beyond myself. As a matter of fact I have to concern myself about the needs of others more than I concern myself about my own needs."

I have to break out of the idea that God only wants to bless me. God is calling me to look beyond myself. As a matter of fact I have to concern myself about the needs of others more than I concern myself about my own needs.

—Tony Campolo

Allowing Faith to Work

The Bible talks about how faith works through love. It also states that if we have faith to move mountains but do not have love, that faith does not help.

I see faith as pearls on a strand. The strand is called love. Without the strand, the pearls can still be beautiful, but they are less useful and end up not fulfilling their ultimate purpose.

For a long time I had difficulty explaining why so many people I met in my career and at my place of worship failed despite having great faith. I understood only when I saw this truth: faith fails where there is no love, but love never fails.

Recently I read about love in action. Bob Conconi recovered from throat cancer, the same cancer that had killed his father, and wanted to do something to help others. Bob had built a custom home on Pender Island, British Columbia, during the time of his father's departure from this planet. To show their gratitude and love after Bob survived his own encounter with cancer, Bob and his wife decided to auction off this marvelous property to raise money for cancer research. This story in the paper reminded me once again that I would rather see a sermon than hear one.

> **Where there is no love, faith will fail, but love never fails.**

Spirituality and Faith Overlap

After going through a season of unexpected turbulence recently, I had the opportunity to meditate one morning after a very long run about where spirituality and faith overlap. I compiled a random list of lessons I've personally learned. My hope is that this list may serve you wherever you may find yourself—*in* turbulent times, just coming *out* of struggles, or about to *enter* a brand-new set of struggles.

Surrender: Do not resist a higher power, but trust the way your life is being directed by a God who is faithful, loving, and in consistent control. We simply do not have the skills to see the bigger picture with our limited intellect.

Being still: Stop asking too many questions. Cease battling, and detach from the outcome. Allow a divine power to control things that are not under your control. Trust like a young child. Don't allow pressure to build up

Passing tests: They have a purpose; thus you will be tested over and over *until* you pass.

Problems: They pass eventually. Seasons come and go; they have a divine purpose.

Destiny: Let God lead, and by doing so, fulfill your purpose. There is a reason you are still alive.

Already: You already have in you what you need to "run your race."

Persistence: Do everything with calm patience, understanding that there are situations that you cannot control. Trust that in the end all will be well.

Patience: Staying in faith requires patience, but it pays off in the long run. Be open to overcome with the support of a power greater than yourself. Do not get weary. Stay in the game. Never give up or become cynical.

Closed doors: These are closed on purpose by God for reasons you may not understand. Surrender to the fact that you do not have 100 percent control over everything and that a detachment from the ultimate outcome produces unconditional happiness.

Timing: There are no coincidences; synchronistic timing is always perfect and divine. Trust God's timetable—not yours.

Affirmations: Declare these daily, calling things that are not as if they are. To affirm yourself is not selfish as long as you match affirmations about yourself with what your creator says about you. You were created in His image.

Growth: This is a lifelong task; stretch always. Enlightenment and awareness will follow as long as you stay open to transformation. Never stay stuck in a place of not moving forward. Character is developed in dark times.

Angels: They help and protect you. They are ministering spirits ready to serve.

Peace: Ultimately, to be at peace 24-7 will enable you to move forward; seek that perfect peace. Staying connected to the divine provides real peace that surpasses understanding.

Forgiveness: Move on; let it go; get over it; avoid bitterness. Don't dwell on negative hurts.

Gratitude: Be grateful for both negative and positive; sand in an oyster becomes a pearl. At first chronic irritation may seem to be negative, but when we look back it is actually a positive.

Service: Love others by serving them, supporting them, and encouraging them.

Miracles: Expect and attract them. You may not see how, but God knows how. (The goal of this chapter is not to define or debate miracles. We could argue if miracles exist, but to those who have *experienced* miracles, there can be no argument. For example, a person whose cancer resolved in a manner inexplicable by a top cancer specialist will see this as a miracle.)

Competition: Be your best, and run your own race. Follow your own calling, and remain authentic and sincere.

It is hard to move forward when we are not learning lessons. These are the lessons I've learned from overcoming suffering, afflictions, and struggles. I would *not* have been awakened to the above list if none of the following unexpected problems had manifested in a span of *less* than three years: My dad died of pancreatic cancer. My son was expelled from his junior high school. Even though I was the most qualified and experienced for a job at an academic hospital, interviewers rejected my contributions. A national newspaper decided to end the health columns I'd written for them every week over two years. My marathon running was briefly set back because of a major tear of my hamstring muscle. A popular radio show I'd done for seven years decided that my segment with them was over. They did not inform me directly but I discovered that they decided to advertise the position I had, asking for new applicants to that role. My wife suffered from a potentially fatal heart condition and was fitted with a pacemaker and defibrillator. My dog needed three separate surgeries to repair both her hind legs and a broken tooth. My expenses climbed excessively due to broken-down appliances all within a few weeks. A very close family member needed to get help from a psychologist for suicidal thoughts; he even *attempted* suicide but survived and responded to in-hospital treatment. Our basement got flooded, and after decades of perfect dental health I needed major dental repairs.

I now see how suffering has the potential to increase our capacity to show more compassion. Like resistance training strengthens our muscles, suffering can make our *mental* muscles stronger. Overcoming afflictions and reframing our problems as opportunities can help us grow. We become not only more spiritual but also more grounded, and as a result we become better able to help others move forward.

It was a season of constant shifts. I experienced many calls to innovate and learn lessons needed in order to move forward and help others do the same. I was learning lessons that changed my life and enabled me to move on. I was purposefully pruned to produce more fruit. Faith sustained me though each of these afflictions, and my trust in a loving God delivered me from them all. Without faith as the fuel in my tank I would not have been able to move forward.

At the time all these numerous adversities hit my family things looked bleak. Since then almost all of these issues passed and sorted themselves out. My inner peace continues to move me forward. I am completely at peace with God. And when I read that Thomas Watson said, "We are vessels of mercy, first seasoned with affliction so that the wine of glory can

Peter Nieman

be poured in," I experienced an extra measure of peace that the universe unfolds as it should.

Be at Peace with God ... Whatever You Conceive Him to Be

One of my all time favorite poems is Max Ehrmann's "Desiderata," which was written in 1927, the year of my dad's birth. I see this date and the origin of the poem as symbolic of my spiritual and physical heritage. *Desiderata* is Latin for "desired things" This poem was mostly unknown in the author's lifetime and became widely known when I entered university in the mid 1970s. It has always impacted my own understanding of faith.

Desiderata

Go placidly amid the noise and haste, and remember what peace there may be in silence. As far as possible, without surrender, be on good terms with all persons.

Speak your truth quietly and clearly; and listen to others, even the dull and the ignorant; they too have their story.

Avoid loud and aggressive persons; they are vexations to the spirit. If you compare yourself with others, you may become vain and bitter; for always there will be greater and lesser persons than yourself.

Enjoy your achievements as well as your plans. Keep interested in your own career, however humble; it is a real possession in the changing fortunes of time.

Exercise caution in your business affairs; for the world is full of trickery. But let this not blind you to what virtue there is; many persons strive for high ideals; and everywhere life is full of heroism.

Be yourself. Especially, do not feign affection. Neither be cynical about love; for in the face of all aridity and disenchantment it is as perennial as the grass.

Take kindly the counsel of the years, gracefully surrendering the things of youth.

Nurture strength of spirit to shield you in sudden misfortune. But do not distress yourself with dark imaginings. Many fears are born of fatigue and loneliness.

Beyond a wholesome discipline, be gentle with yourself. You are a child of the universe, no less than the trees and the stars; you have a right to be here. And whether or not it is clear to you, no doubt the universe is unfolding as it should.

Therefore be at peace with God, whatever you conceive Him to be, and whatever your labors and aspirations, in the noisy confusion of life keep peace with your soul. With all its sham, drudgery, and broken dreams, it is still a beautiful world. Be cheerful. Strive to be happy.

I appreciate this poem for its universal wisdom and its timeless advice on how to experience inner peace, but most importantly it teaches how to experience peace with God. This peace is a journey that lasts a lifetime. As the poem reminds us, it is wise to remember this peace in silence, and we are to speak our truth with humility. Authentic living leads to peace, and our understanding of God's role in our lives will vary from one person to another. To me this wonderful poem underscores what can happen when we have faith in God, faith in others, and faith in ourselves.

As this chapter closes, I invite you to take the first steps up the staircase of faith. My sincere hope is that moving forward in your own faith journey with God, whatever you conceive Him to be, will mean that nothing can get you down. And to repeat again the words of Dr. Norman Vincent Peale, "Faith is the most powerful of all forces operating in humanity and when you have it in depth, nothing can get you down."

What has been written so far may have helped you in your quest to move forward instead of finding yourself in a deep ditch, ready to quit. Yet *all* the previous chapters hinge on the final chapter you are about to read.

Action Steps

1. *When considering your thoughts, beliefs, and words about faith, be sure to immediately eliminate religious thinking.* Religion and faith are not the same at all. Because religion is so often based on the traditions of men and women, it runs a higher risk of offending and hurting some people. It will fail. Real faith is authentic, compassionate, and grounded in love. Real faith will not fail.

2. *Spend time with books and resources that will build up your faith.* You will be shaped by your associations and the company you keep.

3. *Reflect on this simple, timeless truth: according to your faith will you see results in your life.* It means little faith results in little results, whereas big faith results in much better chances of success and victory. Make a list of things that you've experienced in the past to grow your faith into a bigger faith. Meditate on this list often. If it worked for you in the past, there is no reason it cannot work for you in the future.

4. *Make faith your default setting.* Feed your faith, and starve your doubts. At some point we all encounter a fork in the road where we have only two choices: fear or faith. One is positive, the other negative. The key is to choose wisely.

5. *Go over faith builders and faith destroyers at the start and end the day, as these times often set the tone and determine the outcome of your day.* Doing this consistently is critical because it will show you patterns of what makes your faith grow the best

6. *Avoid falling into the trap of thinking, I have heard this faith talk before. This is old news; there is nothing new here.* Instead look for ways to keep faith simple, sincere, and almost childlike. Keep it practical. Be balanced. Never lose hope, and above all be a doer of things that will increase your faith. Knowledge alone is not enough; we need to apply it wisely every day, consistently.

7. *Most importantly keep your definition of faith as simple as possible.* I see faith simply as a complete confidence and trust in the creator. Scriptures tell us that happy is he who trusts in God.

8. *Remind yourself daily that all of us trust only in ourselves or trust in an invisible intelligence or higher power.* Some trust in money. Some trust in science. Others place their trust in philosophy, and some elect to rely on the power of the mind. In the end we get to choose if we want to experience happiness by trusting in ourselves or trusting in a force at work at all times, even when we are sleeping soundly at night.

CHAPTER 7

LOVE

Love never fails.

Love never fails ... What a powerful statement!

Imagine if you were to consistently meditate on these three simple words for the next thirty consecutive days. How could your life be different? What if you were to allow those words to penetrate deep down into the center of your being? What if divine love were to saturate the darkest corners of your soul? What would happen if you truly believed that love is always the *ultimate* answer? What if you purposefully allowed this force to permanently permeate your spirit? What if you harmonized yourself with the ultimate source of love, always keeping your heart open? Pause and personalize how these questions may impact your life and the lives of others. Imagine what could happen once you allow divine love to flow through you more consistently.

To consistently cultivate love is to truly move forward on purpose and reach our full potentials. When we decide to filter *all* we do, say, and think through the lens called love, we transcend tradition, race, culture, religion, philosophy, and psychology. All else, important as it may be, is commentary. When I take the time to meditate and study what God, the source, the creator, the spirit, teaches about love, I can hardly think of one area in life where we can choose to ignore the importance of making loving-kindness a priority. In all areas love has the potential to make a difference by putting us in the best position to finish strong in terms of our families, health, or careers.

Rick Warren, the author of *The Purpose Driven Life,* wrote this about love: "Love is the only thing that can change the unchangeable. Love invigorates. Love revitalizes. Love renews. Love refreshes. Love is the most powerful force in the universe, because God is love. It doesn't say he *has* love; it says he *is* love. Love heals what cannot otherwise be healed. Love uplifts. Love strengthens. Love energizes. Love empowers."

When Christ was asked to summarize the ultimate way to live, he kept his answer simple: we are to *love* God, others, and ourselves. I always remind myself that all our fellow humans on this planet—regardless of color, creed, or character—originated from the same creator. This creator loves them all, so therefore I too should love them. We all have the same creator in common. We all are essentially neighbors. Yet many of us engage in racism, discrimination, and judgment. Jesus was very specific when he taught this: "Stop judging others, and you will not be judged. For others will treat you as you treat them. Whatever measure you use in judging others, it will be used to measure how you are judged." (Matthew 7:1-2 NLT) Our main task is not to judge but to love one another. Working as a medical doctor the past thirty-five years has taught me that before I can make a correct diagnosis, I need to get the correct facts. So often when we judge others, we do that *before* we have all the facts.

> "Stop judging others, and you will not be judged. For others will treat you as you treat them. Whatever measure you use in judging others, it will be used to measure how you are judged."
> —Jesus Christ (Matthew 7:1-2)

Let me illustrate how we judge too quickly by reminding you of the story of a man who got on a bus with his three young children. They were out of control, and a number of passengers became irritated. Finally one passenger scolded the father for his inability to control his kids better. The dad apologized profusely and explained that he was sleep deprived and that the kids were hungry because they had very little money. In addition they had just come from visiting their mother, who was in hospital and dying from terminal cancer. It is so easy to look at things *only* from our own perspective and ignore the needs of others.

Whenever I think of someone who never ignored the needs of others but instead looked for opportunities to love them, I think of Mother Teresa of Calcutta. I think of her spirit and her example to millions—regardless of their perspectives or philosophies. I remain amazed that she did not need a passport when she traveled the world. She was known for her actions and her unselfish, loving, compassionate way with those who needed to be told they were never alone.

Mother Teresa, who lived by the principle that faith is useless without action, understood the ultimate purpose of life is to serve. After reading about a visit she made to Phoenix, I can never visit Phoenix without feeling her spirit still there. It was there where a radio host asked her repeatedly, "Mother Teresa, is there anything we can do to help you?" She kept saying, "No, thank you—all is well. I do not need any help."

The journalist persisted until she answered, "Yes, there is one thing you can do for me. Tomorrow I would like you to get up at four in the morning, go out on the streets of Phoenix, and find a street person who believes he is alone. Hug him and convince him that he is not alone." One can only imagine the face of that lonely person sincerely trying to survive day by day, at times in deep pain. The energy of love has the potential to transform anyone. Mother Teresa also once said that every person in distress has the face of Christ in disguise. And Christ himself said that when we love the least of the least we have loved the divine. In fact, not only do we love God when we reach out to the least among us, but we also see the face of God. Victor Hugo expressed his view of love in the musical *Les Miserables* as "To love someone is to see the face of God."

> **To love someone is to see the face of God.**
> **—*Les Miserables***

I think back, with a deep sense of humility, to a time when I personally experienced seeing the face of God. For as long as I live I shall remember taking my seat in a plane at the Guatemala City airport. I'd visited that country to do some humanitarian work as a physician. I sat back and closed my eyes, reliving some scenes forever etched in my mind—scenes such as an old man with literally one tooth in his mouth, a six-year-old boy with a wide grin and a happy face, an older lady with deep wrinkles and a very tender abdomen, a pregnant mother with headaches due to hypertension. Suddenly I was overcome with emotion remembering the words of Christ when he said, "As much as you have done it to the least of these, you have done it to me." (Matthew 25:40 NKJV) My skills are not my own. They were given to me to get God's unconditional love to flow through me to others. I just experienced what happens when we align ourselves with divine love, allowing it to flow through us to those in need.

When I consider one of the best explanations of what divine love looks like, I am drawn to the sacred teachings of the Bible:

> Love is patient, kind, and gracious. It looks for ways to be constructive. Love is not envious or jealous; not proud or boastful. Love is not arrogant, not conceited, not rude or selfish. Love does not insist on its own way. It is not self-seeking or easily provoked. Love does not keep a score of wrongs. Love is not quick to take offense. It is not touchy or resentful. Love is not irritable; not glad when others go wrong, but glad when the truth prevails. Love overlooks faults, is eager to believe the best. Love exercises faith in everything, endures without limit and hopes under all circumstances. (1Corinthians13: 4-7)

I have never once met *any* person in my life—an atheist, skeptic, or negative thinker—who found these qualities offensive. These qualities are worth cultivating. They are universal. They are timeless and full of truth that never changes.

Divine love never changes and never fails …

Love Is Patient

I don't believe it is a coincidence that patience is mentioned as the first quality of love when the Bible explains what love is. Patience is indeed the first sign we look for when we want to grow in becoming more loving toward ourselves and others. So many times when I look back at the way I've loved my family, I can see where my lack of love toward them was in fact me being impatient. We all often feel like warriors, struggling against the negative energies of impatience, but as Leo Tolstoy reminds us in *War and Peace*, "The strongest of all warriors are these two—Time and Patience." Over time we learn to become more patient in our struggles; we cease our struggling and surrender to a divine love, allowing this higher power to take the lead. We grow with God's help as long as we keep our hearts open.

I keep in my study a small little book that was written in 1941. It is called *The Impersonal Life*. It reminds me that God asks us to be patient with others and with ourselves. But this divine intelligence does not ask us to be what He is not. Love is patient, and in *The Impersonal Life* these lines stir my soul and help me keep my own heart open to where love will lead me:

> Yes, I am that innermost part of you that sits within, and calmly waits and watches, knowing neither time nor space: for I AM the Eternal and fill all space.
>
> I watch and wait for you to be done with your petty human follies and weaknesses, with your vain longings, ambitions and regrets, knowing that will come in time; and then you will turn to Me, weary, discouraged, empty and humble, and ask Me to take the lead, not realizing that I have been leading you all the time.

It is indeed comforting to know that a divine intelligence waits for us, watches us, and, meanwhile, patiently loves us with a love that knows no end.

When we make our personal growth a matter of consistently moving forward, there will be seasons when we progress at a slower rate than we desire. We need patience for these slower periods. We should approach these seasons of waiting with the mind-set of "as long as it takes." How long should "as long as it takes" last? A Chinese proverb states that by patience a mulberry leaf becomes a silk gown. Lao-Tzu, more than 2,500 years ago, described patience as sitting by the (metaphorically) dirty water and waiting for the mud to settle in order to get to a place where we see life clearly. Growth takes time, and whenever I see a piece of silk or stand beside muddy water, I am reminded of that truth.

Love Is Kind

I shall never forget the time when my eighteen-year-old daughter Katie had a few wisdom teeth extracted. She was in pain. Her face was swollen. But when her group of friends knocked at the door and delivered flowers in person, her whole disposition changed to instant joy. She experienced the sincere compassion and kindness of her closest friends in an instant. This kindness blessed Katie but also her friends. I observed the happiness her friends radiated, and it reminded me of the fact that kindness that comes from the heart is the *key* that unlocks real happiness.

We often underestimate the ripple effect of our kindness. Leo Buscaglia noted, "Too often we underestimate the power of a touch, a smile, a kind word, a listening ear, an honest compliment, or the smallest act of caring, all of which has the potential to turn a life around." Parents of my patients have told me about how their children's lives were turned around. I may have had a small part in all of this; I may have said something encouraging to a struggling teen, not realizing how much it resonated at the time. Later the parent of this patient would tell me many years later how the teen had mentioned my words of encouragement at home. There are times when we may never know how our kindness may have a ripple effect in the lives of others.

I consider Katie's friends to be wise, because when we are kind, we are wise. Phillip James Bailey reminds us, "Kindness is wisdom." Not only does kindness lead to wisdom, but it also gives us the opportunity to feel that our lives are meaningful. We feel significant, and as Cellist Pablo Casals observed, "The capacity to care is the thing which gives life its *deepest* significance" (emphasis mind). We feel more significant when we support those who need what we have to offer.

Inspirational author Dr. Dyer wrote his first book motivated by his love for others as opposed to any desire of becoming significant. Today, his influence all around the world is significant. His book *Your Erroneous Zones* sold over one hundred million copies. Recently he appeared on television stating that his ultimate goal is to reach a state of divine love. How refreshing it is for me to witness his kindness every time he appears on his weekly radio broadcast. He consistently gives each caller a gift by making sure they will receive a copy of one of his numerous *New York Times* best seller books; usually it is a book that matches the needs of the caller.

What do we do when our kindness toward others is not returned? Emmanuel Swedenborg said, "Kindness is an inner desire that makes us want to do good things even if we do not get anything in return. It is the joy of our life to do them. When we do good things from this inner desire, there is kindness in everything we think, say, want and do." I remind myself of this wise expression whenever my kindness is not returned. It is not easy to do this unless we are motivated by love. I also remind myself of the sunshine I enjoy so freely: just like the sun, we should give without expecting a thank-you in return. The ego wants us to believe that only those who deserve our love should receive our kindness, but Joseph Joubert said, "A part of kindness consists in loving people more than they deserve." This in fact is one of God's attributes: He loves us unconditionally when we do not deserve such love.

The kindest people are those who do not engage in ledger relationships. These relationships consist of doing something for others as long as they are prepared to do something for us in return. Sometimes total strangers are kind to us for no particular reason—even an unexpected smile can make our hearts glad. The Dalai Lama describes this in *How to Practice: The Way to a Meaningful Life*: "Human beings need kindness. If someone greets me with a nice smile, and expresses a genuinely friendly attitude, I appreciate it very much. Though I might not know that person or understand their language, they instantly gladden my heart."

We have the opportunity to gladden the hearts of others by being kind. In this book I have tried to make the point that we all are born for one purpose: to bring light to this planet by loving others the way our creator loves us. When we do that, we do what Rabbi Abraham Heschel meant when he said, "Just to be is a blessing. Just to live is holy."

Love Is Gracious

The marks of maturity and graciousness, according to William Arthur Ward, are "to bear defeat with dignity, to accept criticism with poise and to receive honors with humility." To be gracious is to diminish our egos and enlarge our hearts to become more aware of the needs of others. It has been a great honor for me to associate and learn from men and women who determined to allow the hand of grace to move them forward.

One such an individual is Ray Matheson. Ray is one of the most gracious people I have ever met. He reminds me a lot of the late Fred Rogers who hosted the award-winning TV show for children *Mister Rogers' Neighborhood*. Ray is always gentle, kind, humble, nonjudgmental, and constructive. He radiates love wherever he goes, regardless of the circumstances or the importance of the person he associates with.

Ray is my teacher. He is a great example of what it means to have good judgment without being judgmental. He shows me that when we align with God and allow grace to flow through us to others, there is more joy, peace, patience, kindness, goodness, faithfulness, gentleness, and sense of higher energy vibrating at a higher frequency than the negative, lower energy of our own egos.

It is when we encounter the Ray Mathesons in our lives that we realize only love can motivate us to become more gracious ourselves. I have heard people say, "When I am with so-and-so, I sense good vibes," or "The vibes I get from my spouse are not good vibes." Call it a sixth sense if you will, or call it a gut feeling. But whatever we call it, regardless of our terminology, we all can remember times when the grace extended to us made us feel good. I believe that the unseen spiritual world originates from our source, who is love. These vibrational spiritual energies are not always obvious, unless we pause and meditate upon deeper truths such as the truths Dr. Peale reminded us of when he explained, "Since the universe is in vibration, it is important to be in harmony with the vibrations that come from God. It is important to cultivate sensitivity to positive vibrations from God, the source of your life"

> Since the universe is in vibration, it is important to be in harmony with the vibrations that come from God. It is important to cultivate sensitivity to positive vibrations from God, the source of your life.
>
> —Norman Vincent Peale

Love Is Constructive

St. Francis of Assisi is best known for his humility in serving others in a constructive way. This saint, respected by many for his deeply spiritual way of dealing with life's diverse challenges, penned these words in a now famous prayer:

> Lord, make me an instrument of your peace.
> Where there is hatred, let me sow love;
> where there is injury, pardon;
> where there is doubt, faith;
> where there is despair, hope;
> where there is darkness, light;
> and where there is sadness, joy.
>
> O Divine Master, grant that I may not so much seek
> to be consoled as to console;
> to be understood as to understand;
> to be loved as to love.
> For it is in giving that we receive;
> it is in pardoning that we are pardoned;
> and it is in dying that we are born to eternal life. Amen.

St. Francis determined to diligently keep his heart open to the needs of those around him, and he did so with an attitude of humility and compassion. He lived by the law of reciprocity, which teaches us that to get more joy, we must give joy; we must prop others up in a constructive manner when they are down.

A law similar to the law of reciprocity is the law of giving and receiving as described by Deepak Chopra in his book *The Seven Spiritual Laws of Success*. Chopra reminds his readers, "Wherever you meet someone, silently send that person a blessing. This kind of silent giving is very powerful. Give wherever you go, and as you give, you will receive."

Love that is constructive never fails to honor and respect the divine in others. It is the mark of true spirituality. Religion may be seen by some as irrelevant, but constructive love, a love in which we honor and respect others, is never irrelevant.

Love Is Not Envious or Jealous

So often when we live our purpose in life and do it well, we attract criticism. The egos of our critics are what drive that criticism. They may feel threatened by what we do. Ego-controlled people have decided to edge love out; instead they compete and compare constantly.

All of us have different callings, and to fulfill those callings we cannot afford to waste emotional energy. Instead, divine love stays patient, kind, compassionate, and constructive and humbly chooses to extend love to the critic. It also reminds us that all our callings include moving forward toward a higher purpose. We fulfill our destinies with open hearts, not wasting time wallowing at a lower vibrational energy level such as jealousy and envy.

Remember the teachings of Maslow, who encouraged us to become independent of the good opinion of others. We should remain authentic to our true purposes, doing so in humility and service and always staying gentle and respectful of all of life.

Love Is Not Proud or Boastful

Tennyson, the poet, said, "Who is wise in love, love most, say least." One can interpret this to mean that actions speak louder than words. Seeing a sermon is far better than hearing one. To be wise in love, we would do well to say less and do more. For example, we all have been in the presence of those who boast about themselves, talk about themselves, and seem to constantly be in competition with others. Rather than being judgmental toward ego-driven individuals, we can *choose* to learn from their choices and instead determine in our own lives to walk according to the wise teachings of the Tao philosophy, a philosophy based on three simple pillars of humility, compassion, and simplicity.

The scriptures remind us that God gives grace to the humble and resists the proud. The Bible goes on to say that those who exalt themselves will be humbled, and those who humble themselves will be exalted. I have witnessed proud and boastful heroes fall. It may seem at times as if proud and boastful souls succeed, but ultimately that success ceases, and they run into a resistance that often arrives unexpectedly. They are humbled, and often that humiliation arrives dressed up as trials. Isaac Newton details how the wise physician, God, allows trials in our lives for a higher purpose: "Trials are medicines which our gracious and wise Physician prescribes because we need them; and he proportions the frequency and weight of them to what the case requires. Let us trust his skills and thank him for his prescription."

The Buddhist tradition teaches that there are five forms of pride: pride that comes from your position, from your wealth, from your intellect, from your physical attributes, and finally from thinking that you do not have pride.

It is important to understand that humility is not degrading ourselves; instead it is a realistic self-assessment, seeing ourselves as our creator sees us—valuable and gifted in order to serve others. Our talents are not anything we worked for; they were freely given to us. The higher purpose is to apply those talents in the service of others.

Love Is Not Arrogant, Conceited, or Rude

The famous basketball coach John Wooden said, "Talent is God-given; be humble. Fame is man-given; be thankful. Conceit is self-given; be careful." Why is there a need to take care in avoiding self-given conceit? It is because conceited people end up being lonely and ignorant. It is a deadly sin to be conceited, not in terms of death as in the end of life, but the death of our ability to bring out the best in others. We cannot bring out the best in others when we are lonely and rejected and when people avoid us because of our abrasive arrogance.

For example, I know a very successful businessman who is significantly superior in his skills as a businessman. Sadly, he remains filled with pride and always radiates a sense of superiority and arrogance. He was married twice and got divorced twice. I cannot help but feel a sense of compassion toward him when he spends many holidays and birthdays alone in his huge home. This is why the divine master teaches us to stay humble and to cultivate love by not being rude, arrogant, or conceited.

When we truly understand what loves means, then conceit has to go. If we choose instead to remain rude, arrogant, and superior, we will remain ignorant of the joys that flow from loving others. Albert Schweitzer, who decided to dedicate his life to others working as a missionary physician in Africa, described how our lives have the potential to become richer and happier when we live for others: "Life becomes harder for us when we live for others, but it also becomes richer and happier." He clearly understood as a healer the healing power of love. He never felt superior or arrogant.

The deadly sins of superiority, conceit, and pride will keep us ignorant long enough until we wither into depression and loneliness.

Love Does Not Insist On Its Own Way; It Is Not Self-Seeking

Pope Francis, so named after St Francis of Assisi, is quoted as saying, "We have observed that, in society and the world in which we live, selfishness has increased more than love for others, and that men of good will must work, each with his own strength and expertise, to ensure that love for others increases until it is equal and possible exceeds love for oneself."

> We have observed that, in society and the world in which we live, selfishness has increased more than love for others.
> —Pope Francis

We all are given daily opportunities to decide if we want to be selfish, allowing the ego to dominate, or if we want to move forward, not insisting in always having things done our own way. Love is not selfish or self-seeking. Toddlers are well known for their selfish behaviors, but as we grow in maturity, we learn that life is not only about us but *also* about others. We are indeed born for a purpose to love and serve, but this is hard to do every day when we try to do it on our own.

But we do not have to try so hard all the time to do it on our own. When we align ourselves in partnership with God, whose nature is love, we are able to sustain an unselfish way of serving others. We bring light where selfishness created darkness. It is a choice we have to make on a daily basis. As Martin Luther King Jr. said, "Every man must decide whether he will walk in the light of creative altruism or in the darkness of destructive selfishness."

I have been inspired by ancient wisdom that teaches a simple truth that we have only two choices: we can be selfish, deliberately deciding to allow the ego to dominate, or we can become instruments of unselfish love. As St. Francis said in the previously mentioned prayer, we choose to become *instruments* of love, joy, and peace.

One of the best illustrations of becoming an instrument of love is a story I read about an author who met with a potential publisher in a Manhattan skyscraper. While trying to explain his manuscript to the potential publisher, he noticed that the publisher was experiencing a bad day. Instead of promoting his well-written manuscript, this now-famous author and former psychologist Dr. Dyer decided to help the publisher deal with his issues. Not a single word was exchanged about the actual manuscript. The whole time was spent dealing with the publishers own challenges. Dyer's agent, who set this meeting up, was furious. "You blew a once-in-a-lifetime opportunity," the agent shouted in frustration.

A few days later this same agent called back and excitedly explained that the publisher had decided—in fact he had *insisted*—that the book *had* to be published. Dyer's compassion toward the publisher resulted in a win-win situation. When we think of others, we establish a win-win situation. We bless them and serve them while happiness becomes a by-product of a more compassionate course we choose. I see this as a great example that love never fails.

Love Is Not Easily Provoked

Those who have remained patient and loving toward teenagers know how easy it is for an immature teen to react too quickly in a negative, selfish manner. Teens can be easily provoked. Many go through a time of turmoil when they become irritable and offended easily. They are emotional and moody, and it is difficult to help them understand that emotions either are hot or cold and that when emotions heat up, it is wise to cool them off first before saying or doing something hurtful or unloving.

As a medical doctor with decades of experience caring for teenagers and as a father of four children, I am completely certain that our patience is rarely tested as much as it is when we parent teens. It is not an easy task, and many parents have told me privately, "If I knew how hard it would be to parent a teen, I would not have signed up for this."

But at some point all teens learn that there is wisdom in allowing our emotions to cool off first instead of being easily provoked. Winston Churchill, once a moody teenager, said, "A man is as big as the things that make him angry." Recently I observed an airline passenger, who was slightly bigger than an average NFL football player, get upset. Although he was big on the outside, his anger toward an airline employee diminished his stature in the eyes of fellow passenger who stared at him in disbelief.

Divine love resists the urge to fly off the handle in a fit of anger. It knows that doing so only drains our energy, weakens our immune system, gives us negative complexions, and steers us into the opposite direction of our destiny. One of the great advantages of a peaceful mind is that it increases intellectual power. It provides us with wisdom. That is why Marcus Aurelius encouraged us to cultivate a tranquil mind, a mind that is well ordered, and that is why Proverbs reminds us that anger yields anger but wisdom yields patience.

Love Does Not Keep a Score of Wrongs

In the opening chapter I mentioned how my dog is one of my best teachers. She does not keep a score of wrongs. C. W. Guswelle said, "Some men learn about forgiveness by studying the lives of saints. And some of us keep dogs."

The world needs healing, and you have a role to play. Your forgiveness is your most important contribution to the healing of the world. I read not so long ago, "There is nothing in this world that cannot be healed by forgiveness."

Alan Cohen, one of my favorite teachers, writes in *A Deep Breath of Life*, "Forgiveness is not just a wimpy act of withholding an attack for wrongdoing; it is a dynamic, creative and practical force that has the power to manifest miracles." I would add that forgiveness is a sacred gift we give to ourselves and others. When we do that, we sense a divine peace that surpasses understanding. In my own family we've experienced this peace, but not before we had to learn some hard lessons about forgiveness.

When my son turned eleven, he entered the early stages of puberty. Little did I know what lessons were looming for our family.

Even before our four children were born, my wife and I agreed we would like them to be educated in a faith-based environment. It worked out well for our first child. However, with my son we received calls from this school, a school with a fine reputation, that he caused trouble and verbally hurt other kids. The school insisted that he change. He had never run into any trouble with students at this school before, not once, until he encountered a female student who was a master at setting him up for retaliation penalties. He got into trouble far too often. The school started to become impatient.

When he and another girl did not get along at all, we discovered how this school made its decisions. Its decisions were based on strict rules. My son was expelled. We placed him into a different school. What is interesting is that at his new school he never had any issues similar to those that had caused his expulsion from the school with a supposedly fine reputation.

My wife and I were deeply disappointed in this school. At first I felt anger, especially when my wife cried just thinking about the sad mess that unfolded. And, like most other humans, I pondered ways to express my negative impressions of the principal.

But the writings of a Buddhist monk reminded me, "Punishing the other person is self-punishment." Instead I decided to move on. We now wish this school the best and respect the fact that the school had a role to teach us some key lessons.

Today I can honestly say that I am grateful for the lessons we learned. Adversity has a habit of making us stronger if we avoid getting bitter and instead learn the hard lessons.

We now understand why the hypocrisy of some religious schools offends so many people. I have far more compassion for those who are offended by what they perceive to be a Christian's hypocrisy. We also learned that what we perceive to be wrong often comes disguised as lessons that help us to grow and to help others who face similar issues. We have since discovered that other families also were told their children may not fit in with the school's particular culture and thus be less welcome there.

It is humanly impossible to not keep a record of wrongs, but when we open our hearts to harmonize with divine love, we discover that love never fails. Today, what happened in the school principal's office is like a wake of a ship. It is fading slowly behind me; it does not drive me. It was a lesson I had to learn in order to help patients in my clinic. The mourning took some time. But we moved forward, refusing to allow the negative past to drag behind us like an anchor.

I have also observed in my patients how unresolved negative emotions can hurt a person. Being imprisoned by anger or blame and being stuck in the past can set such a person up for depression and dependency on weak crutches. Books have been written on the many ways bitterness can cause disease. The mind-body connection is far more powerful than we realize. As a physician there is not a single week when I do not encounter people in dis-ease due to their habits of keeping a score of wrongs.

Love Is Not Quick to Take Offense and Is Not Resentful or Irritable

To be resentful is to block our path to peace. Bitterness and resent are symptoms of the ego—as opposed to divine love—at work. The comedian Dick Cavett observed that some comedians have huge egos, which can make them resentful. Cavett explained, "Comedians are sometimes resentful of their writers. Probably because it is hard for giant egos to admit you need anyone but yourself to be what you are."

To be offended easily is an example of the ego being overly sensitive. It is very easy at times to give in to the ego-driven distractions that we so frequently encounter in a world dominated by relentless competing and comparing. It takes courage and hearts filled with love to rise above our critics. A noble person who kept his ego in check was Abraham Lincoln, who said, "We should be too big to take offense and too noble to give it." Today Lincoln is considered one of America's most popular presidents ever, but at the time his critics vilified him. Lincoln understood that resentment had to be released. He knew what it meant to raise his soul to a higher level, a level Rene Descartes had in mind when he said, "Whenever anyone has offended me, I try to raise my soul so high that the offense cannot reach me." Divine love, a love that never fails, is an energy that we should harmonize with when we cannot by ourselves lift our souls so high that the offense cannot reach us. But once again it is not the natural thing to do.

An event that illustrates this took place at thirty-five thousand feet not so long ago. A flight between New York and Denver was diverted to Chicago because of an offense. A passenger was using a device to prevent the seat in front of him from reclining because he wanted to use his laptop. It offended the lady who could not recline her seat, and she stood up and threw a glass of water in the man's face. A fight broke out, and the pilot elected to make an unplanned stop in Chicago to get rid of the two fighting passengers.

As a physician I am impressed that divine love is not only *the* way to relate to others but is also a divine design to keep us healthy. Being irritable means being fretful, fuming, petulant, easily excited, and able to fly off the handle at the drop of a hat. This cannot give us a peaceful immune system or a cancer-free body; it does not lower our blood pressure. Tactitus spoke the truth when he declared, "Abuse if you slight it, will gradually fade away; but if you show yourself irritated, you will be thought to have deserved it."

When given the choice to harmonize with your source, whose nature is love, or to let the ego rule and fly off the handle, the choice is simple: avoid getting irritated easily, and do as Descartes suggested by raising your soul higher so an offense cannot reach it. Why insist on making life complicated when we can keep it simple by choosing love instead of resentment?

Love Is Not Glad When Others Go Wrong but Is Glad When the Truth Prevails

What are we to do when we see the mistakes of others and are tempted to judge them? Christ and Confucius both taught the same idea: treat others as you want to be treated. So instead of being glad when others fail, extend love instead, and refrain from judging. Let us live by the Golden Rule. We are to be discerning but never condemn others. Instead speak the truth in love. I am sure this is what most of us would appreciate from others at a time when we realize our imperfections.

It is interesting that just at the right time, while working on this book, I had a meal with a good friend of mine who is known for his wisdom and his example of truly caring for others. I asked him why Christ taught his followers not to judge yet so many current Christians judge. I liked his explanation. He said that our motive always must be to let the truth prevail but to do it in a way that people understand it is *not* because we judge them but because we want the best for them. For example, when a teen smokes marijuana, I do not judge; instead I share the truth about the impact cannabis has on the teen's still-developing brain.

> **Christ and Confucius both taught the same idea: what you do not want done to yourself, do not do to others.**

Confucius also said that we should speak the truth and not yield in anger. Too often we say things when we are upset; things we later regret. Whenever we state the truth, we cannot allow it to be done in anger. The truth is that it is wiser to wait before we get angry and instead allow ourselves to be enlightened by *the* spirit of truth, whose nature is divine love. We rise to a higher level of awareness when we do this. We bring out the best in others, and we move forward with them, instead of condemning them.

Love Overlooks Faults

The *ultimate* manifestation of love is forgiveness. The more I reflect on the power of forgiveness, the more I realize that when we forgive, we become instruments of divine love. Forgiveness is so powerful it transcends the realms of religion. Forgiveness is not about being "religious." It is far more important than religion. None of us have to be religious to appreciate how we feel when we experience forgiveness.

We all have made mistakes. If we miss the plane by five minutes and another person misses it by five hours, the result is the same—we both missed the plane! The point is that we are human, and all of us *will* make mistakes. But if we know we will be forgiven, we will be thankful and try to do better next time.

Christ used stories to illustrate his points. He was a master storyteller. One powerful story on forgiveness tells us that a servant owed his master lots and lots of money. He was in serious debt. The master had pity on him and forgave the debt. However, the same servant who was forgiven failed to forgive another fellow servant who owed him only a small amount of money. The story teaches me that we want mercy for ourselves but justice for others.

I am convinced that a number of sincere spiritual seekers do not see results to their prayers because the answers are blocked by unforgiveness, ill will, and bitterness they carry within themselves. They have forgotten that there are no justified resentments; they continue to look for faults, and when they find faults, they are pleased with themselves. We all have met people like this. We need to forgive them and overlook their faults! When we forgive them, it sets us free from ill will and bitterness.

Love Is Eager to Believe the Best

Goethe said, "Treat people as if they were what they ought to be and you will help them to become what they are capable of being." Dale Carnegie had a similar idea in mind when, in his best-selling book, *How to Win Friends and Influence People,* he dedicated a chapter to giving others a fine reputation to live up to. We honor others when we are eager to believe the best about them and for them. And when we honor others, we honor their creator. In fact, the Bible *commands* us to take delight in honoring each other: "Don't just pretend to love others. Really love them. Hate what is wrong. Hold tightly to what is good. Love each other with genuine affection, and take delight in honoring each other" (Romans 12:9–10 NLT).

Love Exercises Faith in Everything

When we exercise faith, we exercise our trust in a system of beliefs. This trust expands when we are *in* spirit or inspired. We see coincidences we never saw before; we get from a place of believing to a place of knowing. Once our faith expands, our awareness expands, and we become aware of the simplicity of it all: connect with the great I AM; do it in trust, and you will experience divine love.

When we exercise our faith in all things, we live by cardinal values such as respect for all life, gentleness, simplicity, and service. In the previous chapter I defined faith as a trust in a higher power. By trusting this power we exercise our faith, and when we exercise our faith, we move forward to becoming more loving toward all we encounter.

Love Endures without Limit

A headline in a national newspaper caught my attention. It read, "Till Disease Do Us Part." And the subtitle claimed, "While some spouses rise to the occasion, new research shows woman's illness more likely to lead to divorce." The piece went on to explain that serious illness does not always bring out the best in people. Poor health can upset the economic, social, and emotional balance of a marriage, and according to the Canadian Association of Psychological Oncology, it is not uncommon for patients to divorce in the middle of a cancer diagnosis and treatment.

It is when we get squeezed by the trials and setbacks of life that we discover what we are made of. When an orange gets squeezed, orange juice comes out. What came out of the core of Angelo Merendino was pure love, a love that endured without limits. This New York photographer stayed by his wife Jen's side from the minute she was diagnosed with breast cancer until she died four years later. Jen's cancer was diagnosed just five months after their wedding day.

Together they went through four years of grueling cancer treatments, and their love for each other knew no bounds. Angelo called it a "transforming experience." He went on to say, "With each challenge, we grew closer. I have never been as happy as I was during this time." He wrote about this test of their endurance on mywifesfightwithbreastcancer.com.

Love that is rooted in the divine endures without limits.

Love Hopes under All Circumstances

One story I shall always remember concerns the firefighters in New York City just after the disaster of 9/11. Many of these men trained for the New York Marathon when they were not cleaning up the mess where the World Trade Center collapsed to the ground. It meant that they did their training on very little sleep. Some ran at two in the morning in Central Park. Why? Were they runners before 9/11?

Many were not runners at all; they had no enthusiasm for the sport, but they had the energy to train at odd hours of the day because their motive was to honor fellow firefighters who had entered the marathon but died in the efforts to save lives that disastrous day. These men trained to honor their fallen comrades and wore their dead friends' racing bibs the day of the marathon in November. Once they received finisher's medals, they delivered the medals to the widows of the firefighters who had sacrificed their lives for others. This story teaches me that when we sustain our hope with love, we overcome dark days. Hope becomes the anchor of our souls.

Although many lives were lost on September 11, hope was never lost. The courage of these firefighters inspired many. Napoleon claimed that courage is like love; it must have hope for nourishment. The ability to have hope under all circumstances encourages us. It nourishes our souls. Love filled with hope gives us faith, patience, grace, and endurance—all the qualities it took for the firefighters to do what they set out to do. When love is in us, it means we have hope in us. We keep going forward because of love.

I read somewhere that life's events are all like a number of zeros: without a digit before the zeros, all is meaningless. The digit here in my humble opinion must be loving kindness.

Action Steps

1. *Meditate.* Make it a daily habit to review the qualities of love as expressed in this chapter. Memorize the qualities of real love—love that never fails and always works. Do what Benjamin Franklin did and choose one quality per week; do this in thirteen-week cycles, and in one year you will have reviewed the thirteen qualities of real love four times. The more we hear something over and over, the more we believe what we hear.

2. *Associate with like-minded people and resources.* We will indeed be known by the company we keep. Stay open to learn from all people and philosophies who are motivated to raise the vibrational awareness of divine love. Never allow your associations with those who have allowed their egos to dominate dilute your life purpose of harmonizing with divine love. Calmly beam love in their direction whenever you have to associate with them.

3. *Make divine love your prime priority.* Without love the best positive ideas may fail. Remember that all the faith, positive thinking, and the best positive mental attitudes may work for a season, but without love, even the best beliefs will fail. Faith works by love. I have seen this over decades as a doctor to thousands of patients.

4. *Be accountable.* Since consistency is the key goal, it may be helpful to allow a person you trust to keep you accountable. If the person is honest with you, it may be hard at first, but in the end you may actually be thankful. Allow him or her to meet with you often to see how consistent you have been in living out the love list. It may be difficult at first, but remember these words of Stephen Covey: "To achieve goals you've never achieved before, you need to start doing things you have never done before."

5. *Never give up.* The best baseball players hit the ball slightly more than one-third of the time. The point is that you may well get

discouraged if you try hard to be better at loving others and yourself. But remember that forgiving yourself is as important as forgiving others. Keep on trying—it is the inches you gain daily that lead to the yards. Taming the ego and aligning with love is a daily battle even for the most sacred saint.

6. *Speak carefully.* Our tongue, though small, is one of the most powerful muscles we can use. It has the power to encourage and honor others or the power to tear others up to the core, leaving invisible scars that may last a long time. Guard your tongue diligently every day, inspired by the ultimate source of love.

7. *Cultivate compassion and humility.* Remain patient with those who are less inspired to honor all living creatures. The great master taught us to judge not. We are called to love one another. Judgment belongs to the master.

8. *Remind yourself that love is the only thing you can never do in excess.*

Final Thoughts

After a lifetime of attending various places of worship and reading pages and pages written by a wide range of philosophers, authors, and poets, I have arrived at a place of a deep inner peace—a knowing, if you will. This awareness about love dominates my spirit: If we want to know God, we must manifest more love. Scriptures tell us plainly that anyone who does not love does not know God. God is love. We will never be more godlike than when we love. Divine love is the true essence of spirituality. There is no point calling ourselves spiritual or religious if we are not constantly filled with divine love. When we align with God, we align with the only force who can claim an ever-present, never-changing, never-ending love. This love is available to the whole universe and can fail only when we resist it; if we allow it to flow through us, love never fails.

This insight has become a quantum moment in my own journey of moving forward. The Japanese word for such a quantum moment is *satori.* Satori is a deep state of awareness, a knowing without any doubt, a moment we will never forget. It is as if we walk from a dark room into a bright room filled with light. There is no desire to ever walk back into the dark room.

Whenever we experience the truth that divine love never fails, we experience a light replacing darkness. We move forward. It is with a great sense of humility that I thank you for reading this book. May it help you to overcome your adversities, to increase your energy, to maintain a daily rhythm of discipline, to become more consistent in whatever matters the most, to grow in faith, and *above all* to love your creator, others, and yourself. I wish you much love, joy, peace, patience, kindness, gentleness, and goodness.

CONCLUSION

I am humbled that you have picked up a copy of *Moving Forward*. I hope that this book served you in your journey to learn more about what it means to move forward and reach your highest potential. I invite you to read this book at least three times: first for information, then for revelation, and finally for application.

My intention for you is that you will continue to receive a fresh awareness from the creator of the universe. May this new awareness help you to be *fully* present and to be excited about your future. In the chapter on associations I mentioned how by divine design—not by coincidences but via synchronicity—we encounter at the perfect time ideas that can transform our lives by the renewing of our minds. May this book become such a synchronous moment.

I have used many quotations of famous writers, philosophers, teachers, monks, ministers priests, life coaches, and motivational speakers. Many of these wonderful wise men and women blessed me with an inner, peaceful knowing that all will be well. They all inspired me to humbly share some of my own experiences that have helped me move forward. We all are called to be authentic, yet along the journey we are sent those who inspire us and teach us how to be the best that we can be. We do not imitate them but instead allow them to inspire us. These extremely influential souls are my heroes. I honor their lives.

Christ is often lumped together with these wise teachers who had good hearts and endless patience and who loved all of life. Yet what uniquely sets Christ apart is that he rose from the dead three days after his burial. To me, this historic event is the ultimate example of moving forward, and it has motivated me to continue my meditation upon all his teachings.

May you get to a place where you have an inner knowing, a satori—an enlightenment that living life more abundantly means total peace with God, others, and yourself. May you experience the inner knowing that all will be well and that you are loved by a force far bigger than you can ever comprehend.

I honor your life and how you allow it to bring more light to this planet. May you sense great love, joy, and peace in your own journey of *Moving Forward*.

About the Author

Dr. Peter Nieman is a medical doctor who provides a program of wellness for families based on integrating the mind, body, and spirit. In addition to proving clinical care, Peter regularly contributes to television, radio, and newspapers. He has been featured numerous times on local and national television, talking about healthy living. He serves in various roles with the Canadian Medical Association, the Canadian Pediatric Society, and the American Academy of Pediatrics and teaches as an assistant clinical professor at the medical school in Calgary. Peter runs every day and has completed close to one hundred marathons, including the Boston Marathon twice. He is married and has four children. For more information, visit www.movingforwarddaily.com.

Printed in the United States
By Bookmasters